Starting with Hume

STARTING WITH ... SERIES

Continuum's *Starting with...* series offers clear, concise and accessible introductions to the key thinkers in philosophy. The books explore and illuminate the roots of each philosopher's work and ideas, leading readers to a thorough understanding of the key influences and philosophical foundations from which his or her thought developed. Ideal for first-year students starting out in philosophy, the series will serve as the ideal companion to study of this fascinating subject.

AVAILABLE NOW:

Starting with Berkeley, Nick Jones
Starting with Derrida, Sean Gaston
Starting with Descartes, C. G. Prado
Starting with Hegel, Craig B. Matarrese
Starting with Heidegger, Thomas Greaves
Starting with Hobbes, George MacDonald Ross
Starting with Kant, Andrew Ward
Starting with Kierkegaard, Patrick Sheil
Starting with Leibniz, Roger Woolhouse
Starting with Locke, Greg Forster
Starting with Merleau-Ponty, Katherine J. Morris
Starting with Mill, John R. Fitzpatrick
Starting with Nietzsche, Ullrich Haase
Starting with Rousseau, James Delaney
Starting with Sartre, Gail Linsenbard
Starting with Schopenhauer, Sandra Shapshay
Starting with Wittgenstein, Chon Tejedor

Starting with Hume

Charlotte Randall Brown and

William Edward Morris

continuum

Continuum International Publishing Group

The Tower Building	80 Maiden Lane
11 York Road	Suite 704
London	New York
SE1 7NX	NY 10038

www.continuumbooks.com

British Library Cataloguing-in-Publication Data
A catalogue record for this book is available from the British Library.

ISBN: HB: 978-1-8470-6529-2
PB: 978-1-8470-6530-8

Library of Congress Cataloging-in-Publication Data
Brown, Charlotte Randall
  Starting with Hume / Charlotte Randall Brown and William Edward Morris.
    p. cm. -- (Starting with-- series)
  Includes bibliographical references (p.) and index.
  ISBN 978-1-84706-530-8 (pbk. : alk. paper) -- ISBN 978-1-84706-529-2
(hardcover : alk. paper) -- ISBN 978-1-4411-2105-9 (ebook epub) -- ISBN 978-1-
4411-4247-4 (ebook pdf) 1. Hume, David, 1711-1776. I. Morris, William Edward,
1943- II. Title.
  B1498.B76 2011
  192--dc23

                                                                      2011043044

Typeset by Fakenham Prepress Solutions, Fakenham, Norfolk NR21 8NN
Printed and bound in India

For our students—you know who you are

CONTENTS

ABBREVIATIONS AND REFERENCES

We provide reference details in the text using the abbreviations listed below. For example, (T 3.1.1.4) refers to Treatise, Book 3, Part 1, Section 1, paragraph 4. This system of referencing allows you to use any edition of the texts you wish and still locate quotations.

Hume's works

(T)   *A Treatise of Human Nature* (1939–40), Project Gutenberg, 2010 [EBook #4705]

(**Abstract**) *An Abstract of A Treatise of Human Nature, 1740,* reprinted with an Introduction by J. M. Keynes and P. Sraffa, Cambridge: Cambridge University Press, 1938

(**EHU**)   *An Enquiry concerning Human Understanding,* reprint of the edition of 1777, Project Gutenberg, 2006 [EBook #9662]

(**EPM**)   *An Enquiry concerning the Principles of Morals,* reprint of the edition of 1777, Project Gutenberg, 2010 [EBook #4320]. Also contains Hume's "Advertisement"

(**DCNR**) *Dialogues concerning Natural Religion,* N. K. Smith ed., Oxford: Oxford University Press, 1935

(**HL**)   *The Letters of David Hume,* 2 vols, J. Y. T. Greig ed., Oxford: Clarendon Press, 1932

(**MOL**)   "My Own Life," included in the *Letters*

Others

(BM)   *British Moralists 1650–1800*, vol 1, D. D.
                    Raphael ed., Indianapolis: Hackett Publishing
                    Company, 1991. Quotations from Clarke and
                    Wollaston are from this anthology. Here we use
                    page numbers

(Assayer)   Galileo, G. (1623), *The Assayer*, S. Drake (trans),
                    in *The Controversy of the Comets of 1618*,
                    Philadelphia: The University of Pennsylvania
                    Press, 1960

(L)   Hobbes, T. (1651), *Leviathan*, E. Curley ed.,
                    Indianapolis: Hackett Publishing Company, 1994.
                    Citations are also given for D. D. Raphael, *British
                    Moralists 1650–1800*

(Micrographia)   Hooke, R. (1665), *Micrographia*, Project
                    Gutenberg, 2005 [EBook #15491]

(Essay)   Locke, J. (1689), *An Essay concerning Human
                    Understanding*, P. H. Nidditch ed., Oxford:
                    Clarendon Press, 1975

(Enquiry)   Mandeville, B. (1714), "An Enquiry into the
                    Origin of Moral Virtue," in *The Fable of the Bees
                    or, Private Vices, Publick Benefits*, 2 vols, F. B.
                    Kaye ed., Indianapolis: Liberty Classics, 1988

1

Life and works

The most important philosopher ever to write in English, David
Hume was also well known in his own time as an historian and
essayist. A master stylist in any genre, his major philosophical
works—*A Treatise of Human Nature* (1739–40), the *Enquiries
concerning Human Understanding* (1748) and *concerning the
Principles of Morals* (1751), as well as his posthumously published
Dialogues concerning Natural Religion (1779)—remain widely and
deeply influential.

Hume was the outstanding philosopher of what we now call
the Scottish Enlightenment, the extraordinary outburst of Scottish
intellectual and scientific activity in the eighteenth century, which
was pivotal in creating the modern world. Edinburgh was the
epicenter of the Scottish Enlightenment, and Hume was one of the
leading lights in this "hotbed of genius."

Although Hume's more conservative contemporaries denounced
his writings as works of skepticism and atheism, his influence is
evident in the moral philosophy and economic writings of his
close friend, Adam Smith. Hume also awakened Immanuel Kant
from his "dogmatic slumbers" and "caused the scales to fall" from
Jeremy Bentham's eyes. Charles Darwin counted Hume as a central
influence, as did "Darwin's bulldog," Thomas Henry Huxley. The
diverse directions in which these writers took what they gleaned
from reading Hume reflect not only the richness of their sources,
but also the wide range of his empiricism. Today, philosophers
recognize Hume as a precursor of contemporary cognitive science,
as one of the most thoroughgoing exponents of philosophical

naturalism, and as the inspiration for several of the most significant types of ethical theory developed in contemporary philosophy.

Hume's life

Born in Edinburgh, Scotland's capital, in 1711, Hume spent his childhood at his family's modest country estate south of the city. He came from a "good family," which was well-connected socially, but not wealthy (MOL 3). His father died just after David's second birthday, "leaving me, with an elder Brother and a Sister, under the care of our Mother, a woman of singular Merit, who, though young and handsome, devoted herself entirely to the rearing and educating of her Children" (MOL 3).

David's mother realized that he was "uncommonly wake-minded," that is, precocious, so when his brother went up to Edinburgh University, David went with him. While the typical age for entering students was 14, Hume was only 10 or 11. There he studied Latin and Greek language and culture, and read widely, most likely in history and literature as well as ancient and modern philosophy. He also studied some mathematics and natural science.

The education David received both at home and at the university was conservative. The goal of education in his day was a moral one—to train students to a life of virtue—and this morality was regulated by stern Scottish Calvinist beliefs. At home, family prayers and Bible readings were regular occurrences. Young David also learned the rudiments of Latin by reading Latin versions of the Ten Commandments, the Lord's Prayer, and the Psalms. Prayers were also a regular feature of his university classes. The emphasis there too was on moral and religious instruction. At some point, Hume also read *The Whole Duty of Man*, a widely circulated Anglican devotional tract that lays out our duties to God and to our fellow human beings.

Hume's family thought he was suited for a legal career, but the law "appear'd nauseous" to him (HL 3.2). He preferred reading classical texts, especially those of the ancient Roman statesman and philosopher Cicero (106–43 BCE). After deciding that he wanted to become a "Scholar & Philosopher," he followed a rigorous program of reading and reflection for three years until "there seem'd to be open'd up to me a new Scene of Thought"(HL 3.2). The intensity of developing his philosophical vision precipitated a psychological crisis in the isolated scholar.

The psychological crisis passed and Hume remained intent on developing his "new Scene of Thought." He settled on a plan that he kept to for most of his life. As a second son, his inheritance was meager. To pursue his goal of being a "Scholar & Philosopher," he needed to be financially independent and that meant living frugally (HL 3.2). So Hume moved to France, where he could live cheaply, and finally settled in La Flèche, a sleepy village in Anjou best known for its Jesuit college. Here he read French and other continental authors. He also occasionally baited the Jesuits with arguments attacking their religious beliefs. By this time, Hume had not only rejected the religious beliefs with which he was raised, but was also opposed to established religion in general, an opposition that remained a constant in his life. Between 1734 and 1737, he drafted *A Treatise of Human Nature*. Hume was only 23 when he began writing one of his most important works and one of the most influential philosophical books written in English.

Hume returned to England in 1737 to ready the *Treatise* for the press. In hopes of receiving the favorable opinion of a leading philosopher and theologian, he deleted portions of his manuscript, "castrating" his controversial discussion of miracles, along with other "nobler parts" (HL 6.2). Book I, "Of the Understanding," and Book II, "Of the Passions," appeared anonymously in 1739. The next year saw the publication of Book III, "Of Morals," as well as his anonymous *Abstract* of Books I and II, which features a clear, succinct account of "one simple argument" concerning causation and the formation of belief (Abstract Preface 4).

The *Treatise* was no literary sensation, but it didn't fall "*dead-born from the press*," as Hume disappointedly described its reception. Despite his deletions, the *Treatise* attracted enough of a "Murmur among the Zealots"—religious fanatics—to fuel his lifelong reputation as an atheist and a skeptic (MOL 6).

Although Hume devoted most of his life to "literary pursuits and occupations," from time to time he made forays into the wider world (MOL 1). In 1734, after his mental crisis, he worked briefly as a clerk for a sugar merchant, but found the "scene totally unsuitable" (MOL 4). In 1745, he accepted a position as a tutor for a young nobleman, only to discover that his charge was insane.

A year later he became secretary to his cousin, Lieutenant General James St Clair, eventually accompanying him on an extended diplomatic mission in Austria and Italy. As he proudly reports in his autobiography: "I then wore the uniform of an officer" (MOL 7). In 1754, he took up the post of librarian to the Faculty of Advocates at the law library in Edinburgh.

Hume also held several other diplomatic posts. In 1763, he served as the private secretary to the British Ambassador to France. During his three-year stay in Paris, he became Secretary to the Embassy, and eventually its *chargé d'affaires*. He served one year (1767–8) as an Under-Secretary of State in London.

Hume's reputation as an atheist and skeptic dogged him throughout his life. Twice turned down for professorships, he never held an academic post. Even as a librarian, Hume managed to arouse the anger of the "zealots." One of his orders for several "indecent" books prompted a move for his dismissal and an unsuccessful attempt to excommunicate him. The library's trustees canceled his order for the offending volumes, but let him remain as librarian. His friends and printers persuaded him to hold off publishing some of his more controversial writings, especially those on religion, during his lifetime. The outcry against Hume and his views continued long after his death. Even his *History of England* was put on the Index—works banned by the Catholic Church— along with the rest of his writings in 1761, where they remained until 1966.

Although Hume's ambition was to be a great writer and philosopher, he was not a stuffy academic. During his stay in Paris, he became the rage of its salons, enjoying the conversation and company of famous European intellectuals. He was known for his love of good food and wine as well as his enjoyment of the company of women.

In 1775, Hume was diagnosed with intestinal cancer. He died in 1776. His short autobiography, "My Own Life," was written the year he died. There was much curiosity about how "the great infidel" would face his death. Several of his friends and acquaintances, among them Adam Smith (1723–90), agreed that Hume prepared for his death with the same peaceful cheer that characterized his life.

Hume's writings

Hume's writings after the *Treatise* fall naturally into four groups. First, the *Treatise*'s poor reception prompted him to recast it. In 1748, *An Enquiry concerning Human Understanding* appeared, covering the central ideas of Book I of the *Treatise* and his discussion of liberty and necessity from Book II. In 1751, this *Enquiry* was joined by a second, *An Enquiry concerning the Principles of Morals*, a recasting of Book III of the *Treatise*, which Hume in his autobiography described as "incomparably the best" of all his works (MOL 10). *An Enquiry concerning Human Understanding* is often referred to as the first *Enquiry* and *An Enquiry concerning the Principles of Morals* as the second *Enquiry*. We follow this convention.

Hume's essays, written for a general but literate audience, form the second group of his writings. They were quite popular, and cover a wide range of topics—politics, economics, history, and aesthetics. His essays on economics anticipate some of the central ideas in his friend Adam Smith's economic theory. Hume revised these essays on and off throughout his life.

A third project is Hume's six-volume *History of England: From the Invasion of Julius Caesar to the Revolution in 1688*, which he wrote during his stint as law librarian, where he had the library's excellent resources at his disposal. Published between 1754 and 1762, his *History* became a bestseller well into the next century, finally giving him the financial independence he had long sought.

A fourth set are Hume's writings on various topics concerning religion. They include his essay "Of Miracles," which he removed from the *Treatise*, as well as his essay, "Of a Particular Providence and Future State." Appearing as sections of his *Enquiry concerning Human Understanding*, both essays were direct challenges to well-entrenched religious beliefs—belief in reports of miracles and belief in an afterlife. One of his most famous essays was only published after Hume died—his "Of Suicide," in which he argues that suicide is not contrary to the will of God, and that in some situations it is morally acceptable. He also withheld publication of another controversial essay, "Of the Immortality of the Soul," in which he argues that we cannot make sense of the idea of an immortal soul.

In 1755, Hume published his *Natural History of Religion*, a study of the origins of religion in human nature. But his most famous book on religion is the *Dialogues concerning Natural Religion*, which he worked on for many years. A draft of the book was underway by 1752, but he was still revising parts of it on his deathbed. The *Dialogues* are one of the preeminent contributions to the philosophy of religion, and certainly his most controversial work. In the *Dialogues*, Hume provides the most substantial criticisms of the idea of "intelligent design" to appear before Darwin. He took great care to arrange for its posthumous publication. His nephew and namesake saw it through the press in 1779, three years after his uncle's death.

The relation between the *Treatise* and the *Enquiries*

The *Enquiries* present a problem for Hume scholars. In 1775, Hume wrote an "Advertisement," which he asked his publisher to attach to the revised collected editions of most of his work. Notably, he did not want the *Treatise* included in these editions. He complains that critics directed all their criticisms against the *Treatise*, a "juvenile work," which he never acknowledged. Seeming to disavow the *Treatise*, Hume urges his readers to regard the *Enquiries* "as containing his philosophical sentiments and principles." When he sent the "Advertisement" to his publisher, he maintained that the *Enquiries* are a "compleat Answer" to his critics.

Hume's seeming repudiation of the *Treatise* in his "Advertisement" and his high praise for the *Enquiry concerning the Principles of Morals* raises a question about how we should read his work. Should we take his statements literally and let the *Enquiries* represent his considered view? Or should we take the *Treatise* as the best statement of his position?

Both options presuppose that there are substantial enough differences between the *Treatise* and the *Enquiries* to warrant our taking one or the other as best representing Hume's position. But there are good reasons to doubt this. Even in the "Advertisement," Hume says that "Most of the principles, and reasonings, contained in this volume, were published" in the *Treatise*. His project in the *Enquiries* was to "cast the whole anew ... where some negligences in his former reasoning and more in the expression, are ...

corrected." He repeats the sentiment that he was guilty of "going to press" at too early an age.

There is another option. Perhaps Hume is not repudiating the *Treatise* after all. His recasting of it represents a shift in the way in which he presents his "principles and reasonings" rather than a substantive shift in what he has to say. He reinforces this option when he says of the first *Enquiry* that the "philosophical Principles are the same in both ... By shortening & simplifying the Questions, I really render them much more complete" (HL 73.2). He comments in "My Own Life" that the *Treatise*'s lack of success "proceeded more from the manner than the matter" of what he wrote (MOL 8). It is not unreasonable to conclude that Hume's recasting of the *Treatise* was designed to address this point. This suggests that we might understand him best by reading both works, despite their differences, together.

The game plan

Hume is a major player in three important debates of the modern period: the debates about causation, liberty and necessity, and the foundations of ethics. Rather than trying to discuss every philosophical topic that Hume addressed, we decided to provide a more in-depth examination of these three debates. After briefly sketching the philosophical background of these debates, we look at his criticisms of his predecessors, his understanding of the problems he believed needed to be solved, as well as his radically innovative solutions to them.

In our discussion of the first two debates, we will often follow the structure—"the manner"—of the first *Enquiry* and emphasize the content—"the matter"—it has in common with the *Treatise*. In the second *Enquiry*, Hume recasts many of the central ideas of Book III of the *Treatise* in a way that is more accessible to a broader, less philosophical audience. However, there are some important differences between the two works. For the most part, the *Treatise* account is the more interesting, innovative, and thorough statement of his views about morality, so we will focus on it.

Before turning to an examination of these debates, we first say something about how Hume conceives of his philosophical project.

In Chapter 2, we look at the revolution in philosophy Hume was intent on instigating, one inspired in part by the great scientist Sir Isaac Newton (1643–1723). In Chapter 3, we briefly discuss the philosophy of John Locke (1632–1704), Hume's empiricist predecessor, and the revisions Hume makes to what is generally called the "theory of ideas." This discussion gives us a more concrete picture of how Hume intends to carry out his philosophical project. In Chapters 4, 5, and 6, we take up his contributions to the causation debate. In Chapter 7, we show how he uses his account of causation to resolve—or better, to *dissolve*—the debate about liberty and necessity. In Chapters 8, 9, and 10 we turn to an examination of his contributions to the debate about the foundations of morality. We conclude with a brief discussion of his writings on religious topics, with special attention to the *Dialogues concerning Natural Religion,* in Chapter 11.

2

Philosophical project

Before we examine Hume's contributions to the debates about causation, liberty and necessity, and the foundations of ethics, we need to look at his philosophical project. The way he conceives of that project and the method he develops to execute it are as distinctive as the contributions he makes to those debates. We can best appreciate his project by understanding it as Hume did: as initiating and implementing a revolution in philosophy.

To see why Hume thinks a revolution in philosophy is necessary, and how he intends to bring it about, we need to situate his project in the context of the philosophical climate his immediate predecessors created. This climate did not develop in a vacuum. During the seventeenth century, as what Hume called (and we still call) *modern philosophy* developed, Western Europe was in the throes of another sort of revolution. We now call it the "Scientific Revolution," which is shorthand for the spectacular successes achieved in *natural philosophy* (what we now call *natural science*) during this period. Among these groundbreaking discoveries were the heliocentric, or sun-centered, theory of the universe, the circulation of the blood, modern optics, the calculus, and the theory of gravitation. Taken together, these revolutionary developments in the sciences created the modern scientific worldview, which replaced the medieval synthesis Thomas Aquinas (1224–74) forged by melding Christian theology with ancient Greek science and philosophy. Since the mid-thirteenth century, the Thomistic synthesis had been the dominant scientific, philosophical, and theological account of the world and our place in it.

Despite their rejection of the Thomistic synthesis, the *natural philosophers* of the Scientific Revolution accepted a traditional ideal of scientific knowledge, which ultimately derives from Aristotle (384–322 BCE). According to this view, scientific knowledge, or *scientia*, consists of *a body of universal necessary propositions or statements about the essential characteristics of natural kinds of things, established by intuition and demonstration.*

The traditional model for scientific explanation—*demonstration*—was Euclidean geometry. You begin with a few elementary propositions, which you immediately apprehend, or *intuit*. You see that they must be true once you grasp the meanings of the terms involved. Then you proceed to prove more complex propositions by constructing a chain of reasoning, where each link in the chain is something you apprehend by intuition, until you derive the proposition you want to prove—a *demonstration*. Although demonstration remained the standard for establishing scientific knowledge throughout the modern period, it was more often an ideal than a reality.

Aristotle not only provided most of the science for Aquinas' synthesis, but also supplied its philosophical foundations. The new sciences of the Scientific Revolution needed their own foundations. Two prominent systems of thought, *rationalism* and *empiricism*, emerged to provide them. *Rationalism* emphasized the powers of human reason, while *empiricism* stressed the role of sensory experience in understanding ourselves as well as the world around us.

In the next section, we survey rationalism and empiricism, and their relation to the scientific theories of this period, in more depth. We then look at why Hume thought philosophy was in need of its own revolution and at the details of his project for reforming it. We will see how Hume capitalizes on the distinctive contributions of the greatest scientist of the Scientific Revolution, Isaac Newton, to develop the methodology with which he implements his philosophical revolution and develops his own science of human nature.

Mechanism, rationalism, and empiricism

By the late sixteenth century, the Thomistic synthesis was firmly established in the Catholic universities of Western Europe. Modern philosophers typically called these universities the *schools*, and those who taught in them *scholastics*. In the early seventeenth century, natural philosophers—scientists—working mostly outside the schools became dissatisfied with the fundamental features of the scholastics' scientific explanations.

Galileo's (1564–1642) *The Assayer* (1623) dramatically expresses this dissatisfaction. He argues that we should abandon our uncritical allegiance to ancient authorities like Aristotle. Instead, we should study the work of the real authority—God— and learn to read "the book of the world," which "is written in the language of mathematics." Galileo thought the proper business of physics is to investigate the qualities of bodies or objects that are quantifiable and can be treated mathematically—their size, shape, location in space and time, and motion. They constitute the reality behind experience. All other qualities—tastes, smells, colors, and sounds—are merely "subjective" (Assayer 3). They exist only in the observer, not in nature. They are the effects of the action of variously shaped bits of matter on our sensory organs, although we wrongly take them to be qualities of objects. Perhaps, at the deepest levels of reality, Galileo surmised, there are only indivisible particles obeying the laws of motion.

The physical theory Galileo suggests in *The Assayer* spread throughout the scientific circles of Western Europe during the first half of the seventeenth century. By the century's end, partisans of this new conception of nature brought about a major transformation in science, defining the framework in which scientific work was conducted during the modern period.

The proponents of this new physics maintained that natural phenomena are caused by invisible mechanisms that are just like the machines we are familiar with in everyday life. The universe is like a gigantic machine. A favorite metaphor of the age compares the world to a complex clock. The natural philosopher's job is to determine how this clockwork universe works—how its parts produce the movements we observe in everyday experience.

According to this theory, which was called the *mechanical philosophy*, or *mechanism* for short, the physical world consists of a large number of very small bits of matter that have only geometrical and mechanical properties. A few quantitative laws govern their motion. Causal relations between combinations of these bits of matter are explained by demonstrating that an effect necessarily follows from its cause. If you know the essential characteristics of the cause, you can derive the effect by means of reason alone from the idea of the cause. The necessary connection between a cause and its effect was construed as a logical relation.

Mechanism was a metaphysical theory as well as a theory of the physical world. Since it presents us with a picture of the reality underlying everyday experience, the advocates of mechanism believed that the theory gives us insight into the *ultimate nature* of the composition of the universe. In addition, mechanism had another metaphysical aspect. The bits of matter that compose the universe are *inert*—they are not the sources of their own motion, so they must be moved by something outside the system. God thus becomes an essential part of the theory as the agent who sets things in motion and ensures that the amount of motion in the system remains constant.

Rationalism: Descartes

No one person created the mechanical philosophy, but René Descartes (1596–1650) was the first to develop it in a rigorous, systematic way. He produced a version of mechanism that he believed would provide a scientific explanation of everything in the physical world, as well as constructing the philosophical foundations for it. His theory became the predominant version of mechanism, retaining its influence on the continent until well into the first half of the eighteenth century.

Descartes rightly sees himself as making a radical break with the scholastic tradition in philosophy and science. Nonetheless, he accepts the traditional view of scientific knowledge as *scientia*. If mechanism is to give us *scientia*, he maintains, it must be built upon indubitable metaphysical foundations. Descartes thus views his philosophical task as continuous with his scientific project. He wrote the *Meditations* (1640) to provide the foundations mechanism needs.

The *Meditations* emphasize two fundamental ideas that guide his foundational program. We now regard them as definitive of rationalism. The first is that our senses are unreliable sources of knowledge about the natures of things. The second is that we can achieve substantial results in philosophy and science by a priori reasoning—using reason to apprehend relations between ideas independently of experience.

Descartes argues that from our awareness of ourselves, and relying on thought alone, we can determine with certainty that our essence is thinking, and that being a thing that thinks does not require having a body. Minds and bodies, he concludes, are two distinct kinds of substances.

He introduces a thought experiment to show that sense perception is not the source of what we know about the natures of bodies. Consider a typical body, a material object like a ball of wax. We tend to think we know the wax's nature from perceiving its qualities through our senses. But those qualities change completely when the wax is heated, and yet we think it is still the same substance. We also realize that the wax can undergo an indefinite number of other changes, far too many to run through in the imagination. The only quality of the wax that remains through all these changes is its *extension*—it is spatially extended. Descartes concludes that extension must be its *essence* or *nature*. Your grasp of the wax's nature, however, is not due to vision, touch, or any other senses. Nor is it due to memory or imagination, which depend on sense perception. Our senses are unreliable sources of knowledge. What you thought you saw with your eyes, you grasped by exercising a previously unknown mental faculty, which Descartes calls the *pure understanding*. Your grasp of the wax's nature is an exercise of reason alone—the rational or intellectual apprehension that he calls *pure mental scrutiny*.

Our idea of matter is not an *empirical* concept, one that we derive from experience. It is an a priori concept, one that we can know independently of experience. Descartes concludes that our concept of matter is *innate*—that it was literally present in our minds at birth. The pure understanding is the only appropriate faculty that enables us to grasp our innate ideas. Descartes finds that we have many other innate ideas, including free will, substance, and our ideas of the various geometric figures. But the innate idea that is most important for his foundational program is the idea of God.

Descartes proves—to his satisfaction at least—by reasoning a priori from his idea of God that God exists and is not a deceiver. For Descartes, the fact that God is not a deceiver means that if he has a clear and distinct idea, it follows that it is true. He now has a logical guarantee of certainty. If he sticks to clear and distinct ideas, he will be error free. Descartes assumes that clear and distinct knowledge of the universe can be constructed through reason alone on the basis of the mind's innate ideas. He now has all of the clear and distinct ideas necessary for the foundations of his science and for the shape his science itself will take. The metaphysical foundations of his physics are continuous with his development of the theory itself. Since his theory claims to provide an account of the ultimate reality that lies behind experience, his physics, like other versions of mechanism, is also straightforwardly metaphysical.

Descartes' partitioning of the universe into two kinds of substance—thinking or mental substance, and material or extended substance—gives him a way to determine the proper subject matter of science. The world of science is the material world. Bodies are the proper subjects of scientific explanation; minds are off limits. With this move, he defines the physical nature of modern science.

Descartes' partition also enables him to determine the real qualities of material things. They are the properties of *extension*— size, shape, and motion. Bodies are matter in motion. All their other apparent qualities are just sensations produced in us by the ways variously shaped bits of matter affect us, which we mistakenly project onto the physical world. This distinction, implicit in Galileo, came to be called the primary–secondary quality distinction. As we will see in the next chapter, it is an important distinction for modern philosophy. Locke developed the most thorough version of it.

Because the essential characteristic of matter is extension, Descartes thinks it can be treated entirely in geometrical terms. This means that natural philosophy—science—is capable of attaining the same rigor in its demonstrations as everyone agrees is found in geometric proofs. Since he begins with foundations that are clear and distinct, anything he demonstrates from those foundations will qualify as *scientia*. Descartes thinks that all natural phenomena can be explained in this way, so he believes that no other principles are either admissible or desirable in physics. Cartesian mechanism is not only rigorous; it is complete.

But not quite. Descartes also needs to determine the ultimate cause of motion. Since matter, as he understands it, is inert, if a bit of matter is in motion, its motion must have been imposed on it by something else. But that motion must come from a source that is completely outside the system, since the physical universe itself is composed entirely of inert matter. Descartes concludes that God is the primary cause of motion as well as the force that preserves the amount of matter in the system. With God playing this central role, Descartes' physics becomes even more metaphysical.

Descartes never wavered in his conviction that scientific knowledge was *scientia* derived by the kind of geometric demonstrations he accepts in theory. But the demonstrations Cartesian science actually produced were few and far between, despite the optimism of its practitioners and their faith in the power of pure reason.

Empiricism: Locke

Mechanism was also the dominant physical theory in late seventeenth-century Britain. But the majority of British natural philosophers dismiss Descartes' version of mechanism as dogmatic a priori speculation. They insist that natural philosophy, to be intelligible, must have a sound empirical basis in observation and experiment. Robert Hooke (1635–1702) speaks for them in his preface to *Micrographia* (1665): "the science of nature has already too long been made a work of the brain and fancy: it is now high time that it should return to the plainness and soundness of observations on material and obvious things" (Micrographia Preface 16).

British experimental natural philosophy consists primarily of *natural histories*—systematic descriptions of careful observations and experiments on a particular topic. Many of them are classics of modern science. They include Boyle's accounts of his early experiments with chemical compounds, Hooke's descriptions and illustrations of how his microscope revealed previously unseen features of plants and animals, and Boyle and Hooke's records of their collaborative work on air and gas pressure. Much of this work is easily recognizable as what we count as science today.

The British experimentalists, like their continental counterparts, accept the traditional picture of scientific knowledge (*scientia*) as a body of universal necessary propositions about the essential characteristics of natural kinds of things. Unlike their continental counterparts, however, they are pessimistic about the possibility of achieving it. Natural historical explanations did not qualify as *scientia*, and there was no obvious way in which they could become *scientia*.

As opposed to the rationalists' reliance on a priori reason, John Locke's *An Essay concerning Human Understanding* (1689) provides empirical foundations for experimental natural philosophy. He rejects Descartes' view that we possess a faculty of *pure understanding* that allows us to grasp *innate ideas* and reason a priori to knowledge of the natural world. He objects on the grounds that there is no basis in experience for Descartes' view. For Locke, "all the materials of Reason and Knowledge" are founded in, and ultimately derived from, experience (Essay 2.1.2). He never questions the reliability of our senses in providing us with information about the world.

Locke argues that before we can address questions about the status of experimental natural philosophy, we must ask some prior questions about our own cognitive powers and limitations, since we are the ones who do science. We need "to search out the Bounds between Opinion and Knowledge," in order to determine "the Original, Certainty, and Extent of humane Knowledge" as well as "the Grounds and Degrees of Belief, Opinion, and Assent." He proposes to answer these questions by applying the tools experimental natural philosophers use to investigate the human mind itself. Following "this Historical, plain Method," he provides what is in effect a natural history of the understanding based on observation and experience (Essay 1.1.2).

The heart of Locke's project is to explain how we come to have the ideas we have, how we should assess our certainty when we claim to know something, and how we should regulate our beliefs when we do not know. It is clear from the beginning that he is as interested in determining the *limits* of our knowledge as he is in determining its *extent*. Being aware of what we are incapable of knowing will help us to be cautious in investigating things we are not equipped to handle, and will reconcile us to ignorance about topics that are beyond our capacities.

While Locke also subscribes to the traditional account of scientific knowledge as *scientia*, his investigation in the *Essay* shows that we have precious little of it. Mathematics and morality are, in the end, the only disciplines that he believes can qualify as *scientia*. Almost all of the British experimentalists' results, and the mechanical philosophy itself—not to mention most of what we consider scientific knowledge today—will turn out to be only matters of belief and probability. But he also shows that, even if experimental natural philosophy cannot achieve the certainty of *scientia*, it can be an intellectually respectable discipline.

Like almost everyone in the modern period, Locke accepts mechanism. He believes that it best explains the ultimate constitution of the physical world, yet he argues that mechanical explanations will never meet *scientia*'s stringent standards. In the first place, our ideas are limited in several ways. We have *distinct* ideas of familiar substances like gold that work well enough to allow us to distinguish gold from similar appearing substances like copper or fool's gold, but we do not have *adequate* ideas of these substances. Our ideas are inadequate because they are incomplete. We do not know the *necessary connections* among the qualities and powers of gold that we must know in order to determine whether those qualities and powers are *essential* to gold.

According to Locke, all our ideas about gold are caused by qualities and powers that gold has, but we know of no necessary connection between these qualities and powers and our idea that gold is malleable. We know even less about what connection there might be between gold itself and our idea of its gold color. Locke suggests that we cannot even be sure that our idea of the gold's color is caused by qualities and powers of the gold itself, rather than "by something yet more remote from our comprehension." To understand how any of the powers of objects work, we would have to know "all the effects of matter, under its diverse modifications of Bulk, Figure, Configuration of Parts, Motion, and Rest." Locke believes that *scientia* is "out of our reach" because we are incapable of perceiving the tiny particles of matter that compose the bodies we observe (Essay 4.3.26).

To make matters worse, Locke points out that we naively think of gold as having all its qualities in itself, independently of other things. But the world is much more complex. Everything in it is interrelated and interdependent. Air and sunlight are necessary to the survival of plants and animals, but we do not think of air and sunlight as part of the constitution of a fern or a dog. However self-sufficient things may seem to us, their observable qualities and powers are due, at least in part, to something outside them.

Given all this, it is no wonder that we do not know the essential characteristics of natural kinds of things like gold. We are so far from having "a perfect science of natural bodies" that Locke regards it as "lost labour to seek after it" (Essay 4.3.29). For Locke, this is simply the human condition. Although "God has set some things in broad daylight ... in the greatest part of our concernment, he has offered us only the twilight ... of probability" (Essay 4.14.2). God gave us the faculty of judgment to supplement our lack of certain knowledge in cases where we cannot have it. Experience, observation, and natural history, not demonstration, give us what insights we have into natural kinds of things. Judgment and probability thus fill the void left by our lack of knowledge. Locke was not only content with this conclusion, he also regards it as "foolish and vain" for someone "to expect Demonstration and Certainty in things not capable of it" (Essay 4.11.10).

Locke is optimistic that belief can meet standards of rationality and that probable inference, conducted rightly, can produce it. In the final chapters of the *Essay*, he develops an account of how we should make probable inferences. This is enough, he maintains, to make experimental natural philosophy intellectually respectable. If we can never have the certainty of *scientia*, that is due to our cognitive limitations and the world's complexity, not to the inferiority of the experimental method itself.

Locke was satisfied that he had provided an empiricist account of all our ideas, and that his natural history of the understanding had traced them to their sources in experience. But as we will see in the next chapter, his acceptance of mechanism, even as a probable theory, commits him to ideas that have no sources in experience. Locke's natural history of the understanding was empiricist, but not empiricist enough.

Hume's project

As Hume surveyed these rival accounts of human nature and foundations of the sciences, he realized that philosophy was still in need of reform. His aim was to bring it about. But to grasp how sweeping he thought that reform needed to be, and what he took to be his distinctive contribution to it, we need to understand where he believed philosophy had gone wrong, and how he proposed to put it on a sound basis. In this section, we look at how Hume conceives of his philosophical project. What are its aims and limitations? What methodology should it employ? He answers these questions in his "Introduction" to the *Treatise*, in the *Abstract*, and in the first sections of both *Enquiries*. But first we say something about Hume's dissatisfaction with philosophy, both ancient and modern.

The sorry state of philosophy

Hume's reading convinced him that philosophy was in a sorry state. When he was only 18 years old, he complained in a letter that anyone familiar with philosophy realizes that it is embroiled in "endless Disputes" (HL 3.2). The ancient philosophers, on whom he had been concentrating, replicated the errors their natural philosophers made. They advanced theories that were "entirely Hypothetical" and depended "more upon Invention than Experience." Speaking specifically of their ethical theories, Hume objects that they consulted their imagination in constructing their views about virtue and happiness, "without regarding human Nature, upon which every moral Conclusion must depend." The youthful Hume resolved to avoid these mistakes in his own work by making human nature his "principal Study, & the Source from which I would derive every Truth" (HL 3.6).

Even at this early stage, the roots of Hume's mature approach to the reform of philosophy are evident. He was convinced that the only way to improve philosophy was to make the investigation of human nature central, since it is the basis of knowledge in the sciences as well as in philosophy. The investigation of human nature is a study of how the mind works. But the insight that best describes what he calls his "new scene of thought" is that the philosophical investigation of human nature itself needs to be *empirical* from start to finish (HL 3.2). The problem with ancient philosophy was its reliance on *hypotheses*. Hume is using this term as it was used in his day, to mean any theory or claim based on speculation and invention rather than experience and observation. As we will see, Hume, like Newton, is opposed to philosophers and scientists advancing speculative hypotheses and imposing their conjectures and fancies on us. But he does not mean that we cannot adopt hypotheses in the sense of proposing general principles based on experience and observation, as we use the term today. In this sense, even Newton advanced hypotheses. In the first *Enquiry*, Hume applauds Newton's hypothesis that *aether* could explain gravitational attraction. Hume's call to reform philosophy is a call to make philosophy entirely empirical and thus scientific.

By the time Hume began to write the *Treatise* three years later, he had immersed himself in the works of the modern philosophers—his contemporaries and immediate predecessors. He found them disturbing, not least because they made the same mistakes the ancients did, while professing to avoid them. Their theories were too speculative, basing their claims about human reason on a priori assumptions and paying too little attention to what human nature was actually like. Everything, even the most trivial questions, was open to debate. Eloquence, not reason, determined the winner. Even the most far-fetched claim was considered plausible if packaged and pitched in an appealing way. Instead of helping us understand ourselves, modern philosophers were mired in interminable disputes.

Hume begins by asking why modern philosophers have not been able to make as much progress in trying to understand human nature as natural scientists have recently made in the physical sciences. His answer is that scientists have cured themselves of their "passion for hypotheses and systems" (EPM 1.10). But modern philosophers, in their examination of human nature, have not yet rid themselves of this temptation.

To make progress, Hume says, we need first to "reject every system ... however subtle or ingenious, which is not founded on fact and observation" (EPM 1.10). These "systems" cover a wide range of entrenched and influential philosophical and theological views. What they have in common is that they are either metaphysical systems themselves, or else they hide behind metaphysics. They attempt to discover principles that purport to give us a deeper and more certain knowledge of the ultimate nature of reality, in this case the ultimate reality of human nature. But Hume argues that in attempting to go beyond anything we can possibly experience, these metaphysical theories try to "penetrate into subjects utterly inaccessible to the understanding" (EHU 1.11). As a result, their claims to have found the "ultimate principles" of human nature are meaningless. In its incoherent efforts to go deeper, metaphysics loses any claim to being a science. These "airy sciences," as Hume calls them, only have the "air" of science (EHU 1.12). They are pseudo-sciences.

Worse still, these metaphysical systems serve as smokescreens for "popular superstitions" that attempt to overwhelm us with religious fears and prejudices (EHU 1.11). Although "superstition" was code during this period for Catholicism, Hume was confident that his readers, most of whom were Protestants, would realize that organized religion in general is his real target. Hume has a variety of doctrines in mind that need metaphysical cover to look respectable—arguments for the existence of God, the immortality of the soul, and the question of God's particular providence, namely, the belief that God evaluates our actions on earth to determine our fate in the afterlife. Metaphysics aids and abets these and other superstitious doctrines.

Hume insists, however, that because these metaphysical and religious systems are objectionable does not mean that we should avoid philosophy altogether. Since these beliefs are deeply ingrained in many highly influential people, giving up philosophy would only leave them in possession of the field. Instead, we need to appreciate "the necessity of carrying the war into the most secret recesses of the enemy." The only way to resist the allure of these pseudo-sciences is to engage with them, countering their "abstruse philosophy and metaphysical jargon" with "accurate and just reasoning" (EHU 1.12).

Thus the initial phase of Hume's project is essentially *critical*. A prominent part of his project is to "discover the proper province of human reason"—determining the extent and limits of reason's powers and capacities (EHU 1.12). He believes that establishing what questions reason is capable of answering and what questions it must leave alone will show that metaphysics as the quest for the ultimate nature of reality is beyond reason's scope. An investigation into the proper province of reason is not just a critical activity, however. It also has many positive advantages, the most important of which is that it can be directed toward the construction of a science of human nature.

Until recently, scholars emphasized this *critical phase* at the expense of the rest of Hume's project, which encouraged the charge that he was a negative skeptic, someone who rejects the views of others without defending any positive position himself. But while Hume is indeed skeptical about the possibility of metaphysical insights that go deeper than science can, he is not at all skeptical about the prospects for a science of human nature. His critique of metaphysics clears the way for the *constructive phase* of his project: an investigation of "the proper province of human reason" and the nature of our ideas, which Hume believes will lead to the development of an empirical science of human nature based on "the only solid foundation" of experiment and observation (T Intro 7).

The science of human nature is foundational

In his "Introduction" to the *Treatise*, Hume emphasizes the foundational role the scientific study of human nature should play in the sciences and in philosophy. He argues that all the sciences have some relation to human nature, even natural philosophy, mathematics, and natural religion. After all, these are human activities—we are the ones who do them—so what we are able to accomplish in them depends on understanding what kinds of questions we are able to handle and what sorts of questions we must leave alone. If we had a better understanding of the scope and limits of our understanding, of the ideas we employ, and the operations we perform in reasoning about them, there is no telling what improvements we might make in these sciences.

We should expect even more improvement in the sciences that are more closely connected to the study of human nature—the other branches of philosophy. The aim of *logic* is to explain the ideas we employ and the operations we perform when reasoning. Hume thinks that many philosophical disputes are about the nature of our ideas. Getting clear about philosophically important ideas such as causation, necessity, and liberty should help us cut through these debates. The study of human nature should also help to improve *morals*, or ethical theory; *criticism*, the eighteenth-century term for aesthetics; and *politics*, the study of the nature of government and society. We cannot do any of these properly unless we know what virtue, beauty, and justice are.

The only real hope for progress in philosophy, Hume says, is to leave "the tedious lingring method" that philosophers and scientists have until now followed. They were bogged down in endless disputes internal to particular sciences or branches of philosophy, some of which might turn out to be beyond reason's capacity to handle. Instead, we need to "march up directly to the capital or center of these sciences, to human nature itself." Before we can hope for any firm and lasting results in any of the other sciences, we need a better understanding of the human mind—of human nature. Hume is proposing nothing less than to erect a "compleat system of the sciences, built on a foundation almost entirely new" (T Intro 6).

Hume's mature project shares disdain for the *hypothetical* with his youthful convictions about the state of philosophy. It also shares his view that the study of the human mind is *foundational* for everything else. What can be accomplished and understood in the sciences, and in the other branches of philosophy, is dependent on understanding the scope and limits of our mental capacities and powers.

The aims and method of the science of human nature

As the science of human nature is the only solid foundation for the other sciences, the "only solid foundation" for the science of human nature, Hume insists, is "experience and observation" (T Intro 7). Although Hume does not mention him by name, Newton is his hero. He accepts the Newtonian maxim "*Hypotheses non fingo*," which translates roughly as "I do not do hypotheses." Any laws we discover must be established by observation and experiment. Newton's scientific method provides Hume with a template for introducing the experimental method into the study of human nature, as the subtitle of the *Treatise* telegraphs.

But Hume is Newtonian in much more than method. The aims of his project and the models to which he appeals to explain human nature are also inspired by Newton. Importantly, he sees that Newton is significantly different from Locke and the other Royal Society scientists, because he rejects their mechanist picture of the world. Newton's greatest discovery, the Law of Gravitation, is not a mechanical law. Hume uses this as a model for the laws he uncovers to explain the workings of the mind.

Hume proposes an *empiricist* alternative to the traditional a priori metaphysics of the rationalists. Like Locke, he maintains that all our ideas are ultimately derived from experience. But for Hume, philosophy itself must be made scientific, grounded entirely in experience. His empiricism is *naturalistic* in that it refuses to countenance any appeal to the *supernatural* in the explanation of human nature. As a naturalist, he aims to account for the way our minds work in a manner that is consistent with a Newtonian scientific picture of the world.

Hume describes his scientific study of human nature as a kind of *mental geography* or *anatomy of the mind* (EHU 1.13; T 2.1.12.2). In the first section of the first *Enquiry*, he says that it has two principal tasks, one *descriptive*, the other *explanatory*. Mental geography consists in describing and delineating "the distinct parts and powers" of the human mind, a task that may appear to fall short of what we expect from a scientific study of the mind (EHU 1.13). He reminds us, however, that we applaud the astronomers who first charted the positions and orbits of the planets. Why should the geography of the mind be a lesser task? While everyone can make some of the basic distinctions among the mind's contents and operations—between the will and understanding or between the imagination and the passions—more fine-grained distinctions are no less real, although they may be harder to understand. Surely, Hume contends, we should not denigrate those philosophers who have recently made progress in delineating the parts and powers of the mind.

But Hume wants to go much further. He wants to explain how the human mind works by discovering the "secret springs and principles" by which it operates. Hume's Newtonian aims are unmistakable here. He reminds us that, for a long time, astronomers were content with proving the "motions, order, and magnitude of the heavenly bodies." But then a "philosopher"—Newton, of course—went beyond them, determining "the laws and forces, by which the revolutions of the planets are governed and directed" (EHU 1.15). Newton's example led other natural philosophers to similar explanatory successes. Hume is certain that he will be equally successful in finding the fundamental laws that govern our minds.

As the fledgling Newton of the moral sciences, Hume wants to find a set of laws that explain how the mind's contents—*perceptions*, as he calls them—come and go and how simple perceptions combine to form complex perceptions in ways that explain human thought, belief, feeling, and sentiment. In particular, he wants to explain the origin of our ideas and the generation of our passions and sentiments. In *Treatise* 1.1.1 and Sections 2 and 3 of the first *Enquiry*, Hume lays out the basic machinery for his study of the mind. He offers a general theory of the mind and a set of laws—the laws of association—that he believes will explain how the mind works. In Book I of the *Treatise*, he takes this general theory of the mind and the laws of association to show how we come to have ideas of space, time, causality, identity, and other philosophically important ideas. In Book II, he appeals to the same laws to explain how we come to experience the passions of love and hatred, pride and humility, as well as fear and hope, grief and joy. In Book III, he applies these laws to show how we arrive at moral ideas. One important advantage of Hume's approach is that it enables him to provide a unified account of the mind.

He explicitly models his account of the fundamental principles of the mind's operations—the principles of association—on Newton's idea of gravitational attraction. The fact that he conceives of these laws as a kind of attraction among perceptions will have important implications for the way in which he thinks the mind operates in acquiring ideas and generating passions and sentiments. In the next chapter, we explain in more detail the laws of association and the implications of taking Newton's idea of gravitational attraction as their model.

Newton's influence and example are evident in Hume's determination to apply the "experimental method" to the scientific study of human nature. Convinced that the only way to understand how our minds work is by carefully and cautiously observing the ways different circumstances and situations affect human life, he promises "to draw no conclusion but where authorized by experience" (Abstract 2).

In his introduction to *An Enquiry concerning the Principles of Morals*, Hume provides a succinct account of the way he applies the Newtonian method. He says he will follow "a very simple method" that he believes will bring about a transformation in the study of human nature similar to the Newtonian reformation recently achieved in natural philosophy. Some natural philosophers have cured themselves of their "passion for hypotheses and systems," and the results have been spectacular. To make parallel progress in the moral sciences, we should "reject every system ... however subtile or ingenious, which is not founded on fact and obser-vation," and accept only arguments derived from experience. When we inquire about human nature, since we are asking "a question of fact, not of abstract science," we must rely on experience and observation (EPM 1.10). He is confident that we can expect success in studying the mind by employing the experimental method.

Newton's achievement was that he was able to explain diverse and complicated physical phenomena in terms of a few general, perhaps even universal, principles. Hume wants to do the same for the study of the human mind. Like Newton, he proposes to explain "all effects from the simplest and fewest causes" (T Intro 8). He predicts that if he pursues his study of the mind with the same caution that Newton displayed in studying gravitational attraction, he will be able to provide an equally economical explanation of how the human mind works. It is likely that one "principle of the mind depends on another" and that this principle in turn may be brought under another principle that is "more general and universal" (EHU 1.15). Hume cautions us that while he will try to find the most general principles, rendering them as universal as possible, all of his explanations must be based completely in experience.

Hume recognizes that his scientific study of human nature has certain limitations, which stem from his empiricist conception of philosophy. One is that although we should try to reduce the number of principles we need to explain the mind's operations to the fewest and simplest possible, we can never be sure we have arrived at the most fundamental principles. Since his claim that the laws of association are the laws that explain the operations of the mind is an empirical claim, he cannot prove conclusively that they are in fact the most fundamental laws. It may well be the case that even more fundamental principles will be found. But the more diverse phenomena that his principles are able to explain, the more confidence we will have that these in fact are the laws that govern the workings of the mind.

Another limitation is that Hume thinks it is important to recognize when to stop our inquiries. As an empirical enterprise, philosophy itself is bound by experience. Although we cannot go beyond experience in our philosophical investigations, this is not a defect in the science of human nature. The same thing is true of all the sciences: "None of them can go beyond experience, or establish any principles which are not founded on that authority" (T Intro 10). All explanations must come to an end somewhere. When we see that we have "arriv'd at the utmost extent of human reason, we sit down contented." When we have reached that point, the only reason we can give for our most general principles is "our experience of their reality" (T Intro 9).

Hume also thinks that as a scientist of human nature, his job is confined to providing an explanation of how the human mind works, rather than trying to make us think better or act morally. Using one of his favorite analogies, he compares his job to an anatomist's. An anatomist wants to provide an accurate description of the different parts of the human body, down to its smallest elements, showing the reality beneath the surface, which may be "hideous and disagreeable" (EHU 1.8). The painter, by contrast, uses rich and vivid colors to draw the most graceful and engaging portraits of human beings. The anatomist, however, is useful to the painter, since the painter who knows anatomy can paint more realistic and graceful figures. In the same way, he claims that the anatomist of the mind is useful to those who want to think more clearly and accurately or to become better persons. For example, a lawyer who understands how we reason and argue can prepare legal briefs that are better organized and more effective.

In the next chapter, we look at the general theory of the mind that Hume proposes and the laws of association that he believes govern the mind's operations. In subsequent chapters, we will see how he uses this basic machinery to solve—or, in some cases, to *dissolve*—longstanding debates about causation, free will, and the foundation of ethics. It is important to remember that his methodology dictates that there is a *critical phase* in which he gives grounds for rejecting metaphysical theories that attempt to go beyond the bounds of experience, and a *constructive phase* in which he sets out his own empirical science of human nature. Sometimes Hume clearly demarcates the critical part of his project from the constructive part by putting them in different chapters or in different sections of a chapter. But he cannot resist criticizing his opponents in the constructive phase of his project if an opportunity presents itself.

Hume's project—its aims and methodology—has been criticized on the grounds that he seems to be doing scientific psychology rather than philosophy. Of course, he would not object to the claim that he was doing science, since his project is precisely to make philosophy scientific. Moreover, when Hume was writing there was no distinction between philosophy and psychology. Psychology, as a separate scientific discipline, did not emerge until the mid-nineteenth century.

Hume's scientific study of human nature is philosophically relevant in at least two ways. First, he believes that we will understand our perceptions—ideas, passions, and sentiments—if we understand how they are generated. As we will see, he thinks that the analysis of an idea—determining what content it has—is inseparable from an account of its origin. Many philosophical disputes turn on the question of how an idea is to be analyzed; Hume thinks his scientific work will provide us with the tools to cut through these disputes. Second, he thinks that by examining the operations of the mind, we can determine what questions are within our range and what questions we must leave alone. Hume, of course, believes that metaphysical questions—questions about the ultimate nature of reality—are out of our range.

3

Account of the mind

Hume believes that if he adopts the same caution Newton displayed in developing his physics, he will be able to provide an equally economical naturalistic explanation of how our minds work. To do so, he introduces the minimal amount of machinery he thinks is necessary to account for the mind's operations. Each piece of machinery is warranted by our experience of the way our minds work. He uses this *mental machinery* as the basis for his critical and constructive contributions to the debates he inherits from his predecessors and contemporaries concerning our ideas of causation, liberty and necessity, and moral good and evil. The early modern period was the heyday of the investigation of these and other philosophically contested ideas. Hume enters these debates with the aim of settling them by getting clear, once and for all, about the content or meaning of the key ideas involved.

Every modern philosopher held some version of what came to be called *the theory of ideas*—the view that we immediately perceive certain mental entities called *ideas*, but do not have direct access to physical objects. Hume holds an *empiricist* version of the theory of ideas; he thinks that everything we know and believe is ultimately traceable to experience. Since his theory is superficially similar to Locke's, scholars often assume that he uncritically takes over Locke's account. A closer look, however, reveals that Hume's version of the theory is significantly different. The differences between them make it possible for Hume to criticize the metaphysical commitments of Locke's theory while avoiding them in his own account. In this chapter, we first look briefly at

Locke's theory of ideas, and then in more detail at Hume's version of the theory.

Locke's theory of ideas

Locke's account of the theory of ideas is designed to counter what he regards as the unintelligible speculative excesses of Descartes' and other rationalists' versions of the theory and the uses to which they put them. He begins with the empiricist premise that *experience* supplies us with ideas, which are all the *materials* of thinking, both about external objects and the internal operations of our minds. For Locke, all our knowledge is founded in, and is ultimately derived from, *experience*. Since Hume is also an empiricist, he agrees with these claims.

The kind of foundation Locke provides is very different from the kind of foundations Descartes thought were necessary for philosophy and science. Descartes believed that knowledge must be derived demonstratively from intuitively certain premises. Locke offers a *genealogy*—a natural history of the origins—of our ideas. He wants to prove that our ideas are *intelligible—that they make sense to us*—by showing how they originate in experience.

Locke uses *idea* as a blanket term to cover whatever is the object of the understanding when we think. He uses *thinking* broadly to include any activity of the mind, such as *remembering, imagining, reasoning,* and *willing,* as well as *cognition*—the stricter sense of that term. All these mental activities have ideas as their subject matter. When you *remember* your summer vacation or *imagine* next year's, you have ideas before your mind of the things you saw and did or will see and do. To complicate matters, Locke also speaks of *perceiving* as *having ideas. Perception*—seeing, hearing, and so on—is yet another variety of *thinking,* in his broad sense of that term. He is confident that all of us will grant that we have ideas, since we are aware of them, and that the words and actions of others will satisfy us that they have them too.

There are only two sources of our ideas: *sensation* and *reflection. Sensation* is the source of most of our ideas. We have ideas of sensation when external objects affect our senses in ways that cause us to have ideas of the object's "sensible qualities." Perceiving a lemon gives me ideas of its yellow color, its sharp taste, its oval shape, and its slightly rough texture. These ideas in turn lead me to attribute the "sensible qualities" of yellow, sharp taste, oval shape, and slightly rough texture to the lemon.

Our other source of ideas is *reflection*, which for Locke is the way we perceive the operations of our minds—our awareness of our minds' activities and how they work. We arrive at our ideas of *thinking*, *remembering*, *imagining*, and *perceiving*, among others, only through reflection. Although we frequently use *reflection* today to mean deliberation or consideration, Locke uses it so that it directly parallels his account of sensation. Reflection is, in effect, an *internal sense*. It is like an internal surveillance camera that scans our minds, recording their activities and contents. Locke never questions his claim that we have immediate and direct access to the contents and activities of our minds, or his claim that we are able to read off how our minds work simply from the ideas our internal cameras provide.

Locke distinguishes *simple* ideas from *complex* ideas. My idea of the lemon is a *complex idea*, since it is composed of the *simple ideas* of yellow, sharp taste, and so on. Simple ideas cannot be broken down any further. Once our minds are stocked with simple ideas like these, we have the power to repeat, compare, and unite them, in an almost infinite variety, to make new complex ideas. Locke is adamant, however, that we do not have the power to create or invent any new simple idea out of whole cloth.

Even at this basic level, Locke's discussion of our ideas of sensation reflects his commitment to mechanism. According to him, our ideas *represent* objects and their sensible qualities, even though we do not directly experience these objects and qualities themselves. Your complex idea of the lemon and your simple ideas of its sensible qualities are what are before your mind when you say that you perceive the lemon. Having these ideas causes you to believe that there is a lemon in the bowl on the table that is yellow, oval, and has a rough texture. Locke's reason for believing that there are objects like lemons in the world is that he thinks that this assumption explains your perceptions better than any other explanation. He believes that it explains your perceptions better, simply because it is compatible with mechanism, which he assumes provides the best explanation of the way the world works. According to Locke, then, the lemon consists of a number of bits of matter in motion that obey mechanical laws.

Locke's commitment to mechanism is even more evident when he expands his picture of sensation to incorporate the primary–secondary quality distinction. You may recall from Chapter 2 that this distinction, introduced by the early proponents of mechanism, is prominent in early modern philosophy. Locke's is the most highly developed articulation of it. To explain the distinction, he first reminds us that *ideas* are *perceptions in our minds*. Ideas need to be distinguished from the *qualities of objects*—the modifications of matter in bodies that he believes cause those perceptions in us. The *power* to produce an idea in us is a quality of the object. The sun's power to cause my idea of its color and warmth is due to the sun's qualities in the same way that its power to burn my skin is due to its qualities.

Locke then distinguishes two kinds of qualities in physical objects. An object's *original* or *primary qualities* are inseparable from it, no matter what changes it undergoes. Divide a grain of wheat, and each part will have *solidity, extension, figure,* and *mobility*, just like the original grain did. Keep on dividing it and each part will retain those qualities until it is no longer perceivable. These *primary qualities* of objects produce in us the simple *primary quality ideas* of *solidity, extension, shape, motion* or *rest,* and *number.*

Secondary qualities—the other kind of qualities in objects—"are nothing in the Objects themselves, but Powers to produce various sensations in us by their *primary Qualities*" (Essay 2.8.10). It is in virtue of the size, shape, texture, and motion of their *insensible parts*—ones too small to be seen—that an object's *primary qualities* produce *secondary quality ideas* in us—ideas of *colors, tastes, smells, sounds, heat,* and *cold.* The violet you just picked has a brilliant purple color and a sweet smell, but the violet itself is made up of nothing but bits of matter of certain shapes and sizes in motion, which have the power to produce those secondary quality ideas in you.

Since the objects that produce our ideas of primary qualities are distinct from us and sometimes located quite a distance away, we need to ask how objects can give rise to those ideas. The pillow I just noticed on the sofa is at least twelve feet away, but I see that it is square, with sides about a foot in length. How can the pillow affect me in such a way to produce my ideas of its primary qualities? Locke's answer is that, since action at a distance is impossible, we must suppose that there are insensible bits of matter between the pillow and me. Motions of the matter that compose the primary qualities of the pillow *impact* the insensible bits of matter nearest it, which in turn impact other bits, until the chain finally reaches my sense organs, central nervous system, and brain to produce my ideas of the pillow's primary qualities.

Locke supposes that our secondary quality ideas must also be produced in a similar fashion. Some of the motions, shapes, and sizes of an object's insensible particles affect our sense organs and produce the different sensations that we have of colors, smells, and so on. Just as the particles that compose a violet's shape produce my idea of that primary quality, so too does the impulse of its motions produce my idea of its sweet smell and brilliant color.

Locke's central conclusion here is that our ideas of the primary qualities of objects *resemble* the qualities themselves because the primary qualities are actually in those objects. Our secondary quality ideas, however, do not resemble anything in objects. In objects, there are only the powers their primary qualities have to produce those secondary quality ideas in us. My ideas of the sweet smell and the brilliant purple are nothing but the effect of the way the size, shape, and motion of the violet's insensible parts affect me. For Locke, most ideas of sensation—the violet's color and smell— are no more like the things existing outside us—the violet as it is independently of our perception of it—than the name "violet" is like the violet itself.

With these distinctions in place, in the remainder of the *Essay* Locke tries to provide a thorough account of the sources in sensation and reflection of our more important ideas, including the ideas of *space*, *time*, *number*, *identity*, and—notoriously, as we will see in Chapter 6—*power*.

Hume's theory of ideas

Hume's version of the theory of ideas is distinctive in three ways. First, he classifies the contents of the mind in a way that is different from Locke's. He then uses his reclassification to undercut Locke's claim that ideas represent or resemble qualities in the objects. Second, he proposes an account of definition on the basis of his version of the theory of ideas that will enable him to precisely determine an idea's content. He will use his account of definition to cut through longstanding philosophical disputes. Finally, he introduces three "laws of association" as the laws that explain the ties among the contents of our minds. As an empirical claim, he believes that they need to be supported by experience, a task he takes up in the constructive phase of his project.

Hume's version of the theory of ideas begins with an account of *perceptions*, because he believes that any intelligible philosophical question must be asked and answered in those terms. He uses the term *perception* to designate any mental content, and divides perceptions into two distinct categories: *impressions* and *ideas*.

Impressions include *sensations* as well as *desires, passions,* and *emotions*. Ideas are "the faint images of these in thinking and reasoning" (T.1.1.1.1). He thinks everyone will recognize the distinction he is making between impressions and ideas, since everyone is aware of the difference between *feeling* and *thinking*. It is the difference between *feeling* the pain of the sunburn you got at the beach this afternoon and *remembering* when you were sunburned on last year's vacation.

Hume distinguishes two types of impression: *impressions of sensation,* or *original impressions*, and *impressions of reflection*, or *secondary impressions*. Impressions of sensation include all the experiences we get from our senses—sounds, smells, tastes, and so on—as well as the sensations of pain and pleasure. Hume says they arise in us "originally, from unknown causes" (T 1.1.2.1). Trying to determine their ultimate causes would take us beyond anything we can experience. Their investigation is not a proper subject for a scientist of human nature.

Impressions of reflection include our desires, emotions, passions, and sentiments. They are essentially reactions or responses to ideas. When you remember last year's painful sunburn, your memories are ideas, copies of the original impressions you had when the sunburn occurred—of the sun's heat, your red, burned skin, and the pain you felt for days afterward. Recalling those ideas as you set out for this year's vacation causes you to *fear* that you will get a similar sunburn, to *hope* that you won't get one, and to *desire* strongly to take the proper precautions to avoid overexposure to the sun.

Perceptions—both impressions and ideas—may be either *simple* or *complex*. Hume's distinction parallels Locke's. Complex impressions are made up of a group of simple impressions. My impression of the violet I just picked is complex. Among the ways it affects my senses are its brilliant purple color and its sweet smell. I can separate and distinguish its color and smell from the rest of my impressions of the violet. Its color and smell are simple impressions. They cannot be broken down further, because they have no component parts. Complex ideas are composed of simple ideas.

One way Hume distinguishes impressions and ideas is in terms of their degree of *force* and *vivacity*. Impressions are more forceful and vivacious than ideas. Look at this ripe tomato. Your impression of its bright red color is as vivid as anything could be. Now remember last year's tomatoes. They were just as vivid when you were looking at them last year, but today your idea of them is much less vivid than your impressions of the tomato in front of you. Last year's tomatoes were exactly the same color as this year's, so the difference cannot be that they are different shades of red. The difference must lie in the sharpness, clarity, and brightness of your impressions—their force and vivacity. This is Hume's initial way of reinforcing the perceived differences between impressions and ideas. Later, we will see that he tries other ways of characterizing the difference. In the end, he was not completely satisfied with any of his attempts, yet they work well enough to give us a handle on the felt differences between impressions and ideas.

Hume also makes clear that in distinguishing impressions and ideas in terms of their relative force and vivacity, he is pointing out something that is generally true of them as a matter of fact. On occasion, he notes, our ideas may approach the force and vivacity of impressions, such as in our dreams or when we have a high fever. But these are exceptions that prove the—empirical—rule. In general, impressions and ideas are so different that no one can deny the distinction.

At first sight, Hume tells us, nothing seems to be freer than the power of thought, which doesn't seem to be "restrained within the limits of nature and reality" (EHU 2.4). We may imagine things we have never seen nor heard: vampires, werewolves, and creatures from outer space. Thought can transport us to exotic cities, distant lands, and other galaxies. Nothing is beyond the power of thought except what implies a contradiction.

However, Hume insists that our power of thought is in fact "confined within very narrow limits." Our creative powers are restricted to "compounding, transporting, augmenting, or diminishing the material afforded us by the senses and experience." I can imagine a unicorn, but I do so merely by adding my idea of a ram's horn to my idea of a horse. We can separate and join together our ideas in new and even bizarre ways, but all the materials of thinking are ultimately derived from our impressions. As Hume puts the point in the first *Enquiry*, "all our ideas or more feeble perceptions are copies of our impressions or more lively ones" (EHU 2.5).

The Copy Principle

Hume's claim that our ideas are copies of our impressions is usually called the *Copy Principle*. In the *Treatise*, Hume states the principle more precisely, making it clear that it applies only to the relation between simple ideas and simple impressions, since we are free to combine ideas to form complex ideas of things we have never experienced. More accurately, the Copy Principle says:

> *that all our simple ideas in their first appearance are deriv'd from simple impressions, which are correspondent to them, and which they exactly represent.* (T 1.1.1.7)

Hume offers this "general proposition" as his "first principle ... in the science of human nature" (T 1.1.1.12). His distinctive brand of empiricism is often identified with his commitment to the Copy Principle. He presents it as an empirical thesis, one that may be established by appealing to everyone's experience.

Hume's argument to establish the Copy Principle has three steps. First, he argues that there is a one-to-one correspondence between simple ideas and simple impressions. For every simple idea there is an exactly corresponding simple impression and for every simple impression there is an exactly corresponding simple idea. My impression of the tomato's bright red color and my idea of that same shade of red differ only in their relative force and vivacity, not in their content.

Of course, Hume is not able to *prove* that this correspondence holds universally, since he cannot examine each and every simple impression and idea. But he is confident that there is in fact a one-to-one correspondence between our simple impressions and ideas. Hume is so confident that he challenges anyone who doubts that there is a correspondence to produce an example of a simple impression without a corresponding simple idea, or a simple idea without a corresponding impression. He is certain that anyone who takes up his challenge will fail. It is safe to conclude that there is a *constant conjunction* between our simple impressions and simple ideas.

Second, Hume maintains that the constant conjunction between simple impressions and ideas is so universal that it cannot be a matter of chance. There must be a causal connection between them, but do ideas cause impressions or do impressions cause ideas?

Third, Hume argues that simple impressions always precede and thus cause their corresponding ideas. He says our experience tells us that impressions always come before their correspondent ideas, and that they never appear in the reverse order. To support this claim, he appeals to two sorts of phenomena. One is that if you want to give a child an idea of how a pineapple tastes, you give her a piece of pineapple to eat. In doing so, you are giving her an impression of the pineapple's taste. You never go the other way round.

The other phenomenon he cites to convince us is the case of someone born blind or deaf, where "not only the impressions are lost, but also their correspondent ideas" (T 1.1.1.9). Someone born blind will not have ideas of colors because he does not have impressions of color; someone born deaf will not have ideas of sounds because she does not have impressions of sounds.

Hume presents the Copy Principle as an empirical thesis. He emphasizes this point by offering "one contradictory phaenomenon" as an empirical counterexample to the Principle. He asks us to consider someone who for thirty years has had the same sorts of experiences of colors most of us have. He has seen many shades of blue, but suppose there is one particular shade he has not experienced. Hume thinks that if all the shades he has experienced are placed before him, ranging from the darkest to the lightest, he will be able to see immediately that there is a gap in the sequence where the missing shade of blue should be. Then he asks

whether 'tis possible for him, from his own imagination, to ... raise up to himself the idea of that particular shade, tho' it had

never been convey'd to him by his senses? I believe there are
few but will be of opinion that he can; and this may serve as
a proof, that the simple ideas are not always deriv'd from the
correspondent impressions; tho' the instance is so particular and
singular, that 'tis scarce worth our observing, and does not merit
that for it alone we shou'd alter our general maxim. (T 1.1.1.10)

Hume repeats the case of the missing shade verbatim in the
first *Enquiry*. While scholars have wondered exactly how the
person might supply the missing shade, Hume seems unconcerned
with the details. For him, once again the exception proves
the—empirical—rule.

Hume's account of definition

Hume's empiricism is usually identified with the Copy Principle,
but it is his use of its *reverse* in his account of definition that is the
most innovative element of his system.

As his diagnosis of traditional metaphysics reveals, Hume
believes that "the chief obstacle ... to our improvement in the
moral or metaphysical sciences is the obscurity of the ideas, and
ambiguity of the terms." However, he argues that conventional
definitions—replacing terms with their synonyms—merely replicate
philosophical confusions. Since conventional definitions substitute
synonyms for the original terms, they never break out of a narrow
definitional circle. Defining a philosophically contentious term such
as *cause* as a *power* or a *force* is just to substitute equally unclear
and contentious synonyms for it, which sheds no light on what
a cause is. Getting clear about the content of the ideas and the
meanings of the terms we are investigating requires something else.

To make progress, Hume argues that we need "to pass from
words to the true and real subject of the controversy"—our ideas
(EHU 8.1.1). He believes he has found a method that will permit
us to accurately determine the cognitive content or meaning of
our ideas—his account of definition. He touts it as "a new microscope or species of optics," predicting that it will produce equally
dramatic results in the moral sciences as its hardware counterparts—telescopes and microscopes—have recently produced in
natural philosophy (EHU 7.1.4).

Hume's account of definition uses a simple series of tests to determine cognitive content. Begin with a term. Ask what idea is annexed to it. If there is no such idea, then the term has no cognitive content; it is unintelligible, however prominently it may figure in philosophy or theology. If there is an idea annexed to the term, and it is complex, break it up into the simple ideas that compose it. Then trace the simple ideas back to their original impressions: "These impressions are all strong and sensible. They admit not of ambiguity. They are not only placed in a full light themselves, but may throw light on their correspondent ideas, which lie in obscurity" (EHU 7.1.4).

If the process fails at any point, the idea in question lacks cognitive content. When carried through successfully, however, the process yields a "just definition"—a precise account of the troublesome idea or term. So, whenever we are suspicious that a

philosophical term is employed without any meaning or idea (as is but too frequent), we need but enquire, *from what impression is that supposed idea derived?* And if it be impossible to assign any, this will serve to confirm our suspicion. By bringing ideas into so clear a light, we may reasonably hope to remove all dispute, which may arise, concerning their nature and reality. (EHU 2.9)

Hume's use of this procedure reveals that the content of many philosophically important ideas such as causation or necessity is considerably less than metaphysicians have claimed. His account of definition is essential to the way he solves or dissolves longstanding philosophical debates, including the debates about causation and the freedom of the will.

Hume's criticism of Locke

Hume uses his version of the theory of ideas—which differs from Locke's—both to criticize Locke's metaphysical commitments and to avoid similar commitments of his own. According to Locke's account of perception, physical objects with certain qualities and powers cause our ideas of sensation. We do not immediately or directly perceive these objects, which are independent of us. We *infer* their existence from our ideas. Our primary quality ideas *resemble* the primary qualities of the objects that cause those ideas, while secondary quality ideas do not.

Hume's distinction between impressions and ideas directly undercuts the intelligibility of Locke's conclusions about objects and their primary qualities. For Hume, our simple ideas are copies of our simple impressions. They represent and resemble them. We cannot intelligibly ask about the causes of our impressions or what they represent or resemble, since these questions go beyond the bounds of experience. But that is exactly what Locke does. His views about objects and their primary qualities are inferences from what we experience to conclusions about what we cannot experience, which contradicts his own commitment to an empiricist standard for the intelligibility of ideas.

In the *Treatise*, Hume calls Locke's view "the hypothesis ... of the double existence of perceptions and objects," because Locke is committed both to the existence of ideas or perceptions, which we immediately perceive, and to the existence of the external world of physical objects, whose existence we infer but never directly perceive (T 1.4.2.52). He first argues that this "strain'd metaphysical conviction" cannot be established by causal reasoning (T 1.4.2.51). Causal relations must be established by past experience, when we have found that "two beings are constantly conjoin'd together, and are always present at once to the mind." For example, in the past I have often experienced headache relief after taking aspirin, so I regard taking aspirin as the cause of my headache relief. But the "only existences, of which we are certain, are perceptions," which are "immediately present to us by consciousness" (T 1.4.2.47). Since only perceptions are present to our minds, we can observe causal relations between them. We cannot observe causal relations between our perceptions and objects, since objects are never present to our minds. Hume concludes that it is impossible to draw any just conclusion concerning the existence or qualities of objects from the existence or qualities of our perceptions. We cannot draw a just conclusion because we cannot cash out Locke's objects, or their qualities and powers, in terms of perceptions (T 1.4.2.54). The *double existence hypothesis* goes beyond the bounds of sense.

Hume makes this point explicit when he reminds us in the first *Enquiry* that, since it is a question of fact how and by what our perceptions are caused, only experience can provide the answer.

But in the case of the *double existence hypothesis*, "experience is, and must be entirely silent" (EHU 12.1.12). Any experience would necessarily consist of more perceptions, and they can tell us no more about the alleged connection between our perceptions and independent external objects than could our original perceptions. Hume concludes that supposing that there is such a connection has no foundation.

Trying to answer a question of fact that cannot be decided by any possible experience is not just false, but unintelligible. That is because, on Hume's account of definition, we cannot have the ideas that we would have to have in order to answer the question *"Are our perceptions caused by independent external objects?"* one way or the other, or even to make sense of the question itself.

Locke fails to see that he is attempting to go beyond the limits of experience when he develops his account of perception in general and the primary–secondary quality distinction in particular. He frames his entire discussion in terms of mechanism, which he takes to be a plausible theory that provides the best explanation of the way the world is. His enthusiasm for mechanism blinds him to the fact that in adopting it, he is nonetheless embracing the kind of "ultimate principles" that Hume—and ironically, Locke himself—criticize in other metaphysical theories (Abstract 1). Although Locke sees himself as a metaphysical minimalist, he is nonetheless committed to a substantive metaphysical theory about the ultimate nature of reality.

Hume avoids these metaphysical commitments by refusing to regard any term as meaningful or idea as intelligible unless its content can be completely specified in terms of impressions, just as his account of definition dictates. He never loses sight of the need to end an inquiry when he has reached simple impressions.

The principles of association

We are capable of separating and combining our simple ideas in any way we choose, short of a contradiction. I can think of the streets of New York City as paved with gold and imagine my dog with the wings of an eagle. Nevertheless, there is a pattern or regular order to our thoughts. Certain ideas tend to go with certain other ideas. When you think of one thing, you naturally think of something else. If our ideas occurred to us randomly, so that all our thoughts were "loose and unconnected," we wouldn't be able to think coherently (T 1.1.4.1). This suggests, as Hume says in the *Abstract*, that

> there is a secret tie or union among particular ideas, which causes the mind to conjoin them more frequently, and makes the one, upon its appearance, introduce the other. (Abstract 35)

When I receive an invitation to my nephew's wedding, I think of my sister. If I realize that Friday is the first of the month, I think about getting paid. When someone mentions summer, I think of the beach. In all these cases, there seems to be some *connection*—some *tie* or *union*—between the ideas involved. Moreover, in each case it also seems as though the one idea *introduces* the other.

Hume says that this pattern or order is most evident when we are solving a problem or explaining a complex procedure. But there is also some regularity among our ideas even in our wildest and most wandering daydreams. We are also usually able to find the thread that connects ideas in a rambling conversation. When someone breaks the thread of a conversation, he can tell you what occurred to him that led him to switch topics. Almost every language has words that express the same combination of simple ideas—tomato, flower, or sunburn, to name a few. These familiar features of thought, conversation, and language indicate that our simple ideas are regularly and uniformly connected.

Hume thinks that a science of human nature should account for this "secret tie or union" between our ideas, "by which one idea naturally introduces another." He explains this union in terms of the mind's natural ability to *associate* certain ideas. Association is not "an inseparable connexion," since we have seen that our imaginations can separate any two distinct simple ideas. It is rather "a gentle force, which commonly prevails" (T 1.1.4.1).

In the first *Enquiry*, Hume says that even though it is obvious to everyone that ideas are connected in this way, he is the first philosopher who has "attempted to enumerate or class all the principles of association" (EHU 3.2). His identification and use of the "universal principles" that account for these patterns in our thinking are distinctive features of his particular brand of empiricism. Hume thinks his uses of the principles of association are so distinctive that in the *Abstract* he advertises it as his most original contribution—what entitles him to be called an *inventor*.

Hume identifies three principles of connection among our ideas: *resemblance, contiguity in time and place*, and *causation*. When someone shows you a picture of your best friend, you naturally think of her. You are led from the picture to thoughts of your friend because the picture *resembles* her. *Contiguity in time*—temporal closeness—works like this: when you're reminded of something that happened in the 1960s—say, miniskirts—you may also recall something else that happened in that period, like the Vietnam War. *Contiguity in place*—spatial closeness—works in a similar way. Thinking of Sausalito may lead you to think of the Golden Gate Bridge, which may also lead you to think of San Francisco. *Causality* works both from cause to effect and from effect to cause: meeting someone's father may make you think of his son, and encountering the son may make you think of his father. If you are told about a friend's broken arm, you naturally think about the injury's effect and the pain it caused her, while if you see someone in severe pain, you are led to think about the injury that caused it.

The associative principles may also work together to form chains of association. We may even end up thinking about something that is not connected to the idea with which the chain began. Someone may mention Plato, and this may make you think of Aristotle. After all, they *resemble* each other because they were both great Greek philosophers. They both lived in fifth-century BCE Athens, and thus are *contiguous in time and place*. Plato was also Aristotle's teacher, and in this sense, the *cause* of his becoming a philosopher. Thinking of Aristotle may result by *contiguity in place* in your remembering your trip to Assos in Turkey, where Aristotle had a school, and your memories of Assos may turn your thoughts to ancient Troy, which is nearby—again, *contiguity in place*. Finally, thinking of ancient Troy may take you, via *resemblance* and *causation*, to thoughts of Brad Pitt, who played Achilles in a recent movie about the Trojan War. Your ideas of Plato and Brad Pitt are not themselves connected, even though all the links in the chain of ideas between them are composed of one or more of the associative principles.

Of the three associative principles, causation is the strongest. It makes "one idea readily recall another" (T 1.1.4.2). It is also the only associative principle that takes us "beyond our senses" (T 1.3.2.3). It establishes a connection between past and present experiences with events that we expect, predict, or explain, so that "all reasonings concerning matters of fact seem to be founded in the relation of *Cause and Effect*" (EHU 4.1.4). My taking aspirin in the past has been followed by headache relief, so I now expect that the aspirin I just took will soon relieve my present headache. Hume also regards causation as the least understood of the associative principles, but he tells us "we shall have occasion afterwards to examine it to the bottom, and therefore shall not at present insist upon it" (T 1.1.4.2).

Hume compares his identification of the principles of association of ideas in the science of human nature to Newton's discovery of the Law of Gravitation in natural philosophy. Like gravitational attraction, the associative principles are *original*. Although he appeals to them to explain how our minds work, he thinks that they cannot be explained further. Stopping with these original principles is doing the science of human nature right. We should not look for causes that lie beyond the bounds of experience and we ought to curb any "intemperate desire" we might have to do so:

> Here is a kind of ATTRACTION, which in the mental world will be found to have as extraordinary effects as in the natural, and to shew itself in as many and as various forms. Its effects are every where conspicuous; but as to its causes, they are mostly unknown, and must be resolv'd into *original* qualities of human nature, which I pretend not to explain. Nothing is more requisite for a true philosopher, than to restrain their intemperate desire of searching into causes, and having establish'd any doctrine upon a sufficient number of experiments, rest contented with that, when he sees a farther examination wou'd lead him into obscure and uncertain speculations. (T 1.1.4.6)

It is not part of Hume's project to try to explain why we associate ideas as we do, nor is it his aim to tell us that we ought to associate our ideas in these ways. He is interested only in establishing that, as a matter of fact, we *do* associate ideas in these ways.

In the first *Enquiry*, Hume admits he cannot prove conclusively that his list of associative principles is complete. His claim that the three principles of association explain the important operations of the mind is an empirical claim. Maybe he has overlooked some principle. We are free to examine the patterns in our own thought and see whether resemblance, contiguity, and causation successfully explain them. The more instances the associative principles explain, the more assurance we will have that Hume has indeed identified the basic principles by which our minds operate.

Hume's task is to show in detail that the principles of association explain how we come to think, believe, and feel as we do. We will be in a better position to assess whether Hume has correctly identified the principles of association after looking at his accounts of our causal and moral judgments.

In the *Abstract*, Hume concludes that it should be

> easy to conceive of what vast consequences these principles must be in the science of human nature, if we consider, that so far as regards the mind, these are the only links that bind the parts of the universe together, or connect us with any person or object exterior to ourselves. For as it is by means of thought only that any thing operates upon our passions, and as these are the only ties of our thoughts, they are really *to us* the cement of the universe, and all the operations of the mind must, in a great measure, depend on them. (Abstract 35)

Just what "vast consequences" the associative principles have for the science of human nature will become clear when we examine Hume's revolutionary accounts of our causal inferences and our idea of the necessary connection between causes and effects in Chapters 4–6.

Philosophical relations

Hume points out that the term *relation* is used in two "considerably different" senses. The sense that is most used in "common language" is the way we relate ideas by association, where "two ideas are connected together in the imagination, and the one naturally introduces the other." The other sense of *relation* is where "we think it proper to compare" two ideas, even when they are given "an arbitrary union … in the fancy." Hume says that only in philosophy do we extend the term this way "to mean any particular subject of comparison, without a connecting principle," so he calls relations in this second sense, *philosophical relations* (T 1.1.5.1). In this context, he intends us to understand "philosophy" as covering both natural philosophy and philosophy in the sense in which we use it today.

In *Treatise* 1.1.5, Hume distinguishes seven philosophical relations. Later on, he divides them into two categories: *relations of ideas*, which are discoverable by means of intuition and demonstration, and *relations of matters of fact*, which cannot be determined by considering ideas alone, and thus are dependent on experience (T 1.3.1.2).

There are four *relations of ideas*: *resemblance*, which is necessary for all philosophical relations, since no two things can be compared at all, unless they resemble one another in *some* respect; *quantity* or *number* relates ideas in terms of their relative sizes, lengths, weights, and numbers; *degrees of quality* relate ideas by their relative amount or degree of a given quality they share, as when we say that *true navy* is darker in color than *Cambridge blue*; *contrariety* relates ideas by their opposition or incompatibility. When we consider ideas as contraries, we see them as incompatible with regard to the same quality, nature, or action.

Hume thinks that we can determine that the relations of resemblance, degree of quality, and contrariety by *intuition*—by simply inspecting the ideas involved. When we consider relations of quantity or number, however, reasoning is required. We determine these relations by *demonstration*—by constructing mathematical proofs.

The three *relations of matters of fact* are *identity over time*—whether this church is the same as the one that was here earlier; *spatial and temporal relations*—how close or how far apart in space and time two things are; and *causation*—whether smoke is the cause of fire or whether fire is the cause of smoke. Hume argues that both identity and spatial and temporal contiguity may be directly perceived, while causation, which takes us beyond direct perception, involves a process of reasoning.

In the *Treatise*, Hume presents his definitions of our idea of *cause* in terms of philosophical and natural relations, but in the first *Enquiry*, he drops this terminology altogether. The philosophical relations play a role in Hume's criticism of moral rationalism, especially in Book 3 of the *Treatise*.

In the next three chapters, we will see how Hume applies his method and his account of the mind and its ideas to one of the central problems in modern philosophy: the causation debate.

4

Causal inference: skeptical doubts

With the method and machinery for his empirical study of human nature in place, Hume puts them to work on a central issue in modern philosophy—the causation debate. This debate concerns a group of closely related questions about the relation between cause and effect: When are two events or objects causally related? What is the nature of our inferences from cause to effect, or from effect to cause? What is the foundation or basis of our causal inferences?

Philosophical context: the causation debate

Modern philosophers, rationalists and empiricists alike, think of themselves as scientific revolutionaries because they reject the scholastics' account of causation, which was derived from Aristotle. They agree that events or objects that are causally related are *connected*, and not merely *conjoined*, with their effects. Lightning does not simply *precede* thunder; it is *connected* with the thunder as its cause. Smoke and heat are reliable indicators of fire because they are the effects of fire; they are not just accidentally correlated with it.

The moderns believe that our idea of causation also involves the idea of *necessary connection*. When a cause occurs, its effect *must* follow. It is not that the smoke you see and the intense heat you feel *might* be the effects of fire: they *must* be the effects of fire. Causes are *necessarily connected* with their effects. Every modern philosopher prior to Hume assumes that the inevitability of an effect given the cause means that the connection is a *logical* one.

In making causal inferences, we use our knowledge of causes to predict or explain what effects they will produce given the necessary connection between a cause and its effects. Causal inferences take us from what we have observed or are now observing to *beliefs* about what we will observe in the immediate future. They take us from the observed to the unobserved, and from the past and present to the future. Seeing the lightning leads you to *expect* the rumble of thunder. When you smell smoke and feel heat, you *believe* that you will soon see flames.

Importantly, rationalists and empiricists alike assume that causal inferences are activities or exercises of reason or the understanding. They also accept the scholastics' absolute distinction between the categories of knowledge (*scientia*) and belief (*opinio*). They differ, however, on the question of whether our causal inferences yield knowledge or only belief.

Philosophers in the *rationalist* tradition, including Descartes and Nicholas Malebranche (1638–1715), as well as their counterparts in Britain, Thomas Hobbes (1588–1679) and Samuel Clarke (1675–1729), think that causal inference is either a matter of *intuition or demonstration*. They believe that when you have a clear and complete idea of a cause, you can conclude immediately—by *intuition*—what effects are *necessarily connected* with it. Either you can see that the idea of the effect is *contained* in your idea of the cause, so that you can immediately intuit it, or else you can see that your idea of the cause includes the idea of the *power* to produce that effect. If you have a clear and complete idea of gold, your idea should include either the idea that gold is soluble in *aqua regia* (a nitro-sulfuric acid solution) or the idea that *aqua regia* has the *power* to dissolve gold.

When you are unable to immediately intuit that the necessary connection between cause and effect obtains, you must derive the effect using a chain of reasoning involving other principles you do intuit immediately, which connects the effect with its cause. If your idea of gold lacks clarity and completeness, then to know that gold is soluble in *aqua regia*, you must derive it by constructing a demonstration using the necessary physical principles. Philosophers in the *rationalist* tradition were optimistic that we can obtain knowledge (*scientia*) of causes and effects through demonstration, but they rarely delivered the goods. Systematic demonstrative causal knowledge was for them always more of an ideal than a reality.

Empiricists, as well as the natural philosophers in the British experimental tradition that follow Locke, agree with the rationalists that causal inferences involve the exercise of reason. They are more pessimistic, however, about the possibility of obtaining demonstrative causal knowledge. Locke himself, as we have seen, is skeptical about whether we could ever attain any substantial causal knowledge through demonstration. He was convinced that God intended us to live in "the twilight of probability" and belief rather than the "bright sunshine" of knowledge because he believes that we will never become aware of the necessary connections involved (Essay 4.14.2). But for Locke this is no ground for despair, since he thinks that we are capable of using our reason to arrive at reasonable beliefs about our own causal powers—our ability to move our bodies or to call up our ideas—and the causal powers of external objects. He constructs one of the first accounts of probable inference with the aim of showing us the right way to use our reason to arrive at causal beliefs.

Hume's overall strategy

Hume agrees with his immediate predecessors and contemporaries that our idea of causation involves the idea of necessary connection—that given the cause, the effect must occur. But he was the first to realize that there was something seriously wrong with their attempts to account for this idea. Instead of first attempting to analyze the idea of necessary connection, however, he begins by examining the causal inferences we make. Hume adopts this strategy because he is convinced that in order to understand our idea of necessary connection, we first need to understand the nature of our causal inferences. His insight is that the nature of the relation depends on the nature of the inference, and not the other way round, as his predecessors thought.

Hume's method dictates his strategy. He first looks at our causal inferences. In the *critical phase* of his account, he argues that his rationalist and empiricist predecessors were wrong: Our causal inferences are *not* determined by "any argument or process of the understanding" (EHU 5.1.2). Hume supplies an alternative understanding of causal inference in his *constructive phase*: He argues that the associative principles are the basis of our causal inferences. He is then ready to examine our idea of *necessary connection*. He agrees with his predecessors that necessary connection is an essential part of our idea of causation. In the *critical phase*, he argues that the various attempts to characterize the idea of necessary connection are unintelligible. In the *constructive phase*, he offers his own positive account of that idea, by determining its source in impressions. His discussion culminates with his definition of our idea of *cause*.

Hume's contributions to the *critical phase* of our idea of causal inference are contained in *Treatise* 1.3.6 and in Section 4 of the first *Enquiry*, the appropriately titled "Sceptical doubts concerning the operations of the understanding." The critical phase of his account is the subject of the present chapter. His two critical discussions of causal inference differ in detail, but not in substance. Our version of his argument is a hybrid that closely follows his presentation in the first *Enquiry*, where its structure is straightforward, which we supplement with passages from the *Treatise* and the *Abstract*.

The *constructive phase* of his account of causal inference in the *Enquiry* is in Section 5, also appropriately titled "Sceptical solution of these doubts," while the *constructive phase* in the *Treatise* stretches from 1.3.7 through 1.3.10. We will examine the constructive aspect of his account of causal inference in the next chapter. His *critical* and *constructive accounts* of our idea of necessary connection are found in single sections of both works: *Enquiry* 7 and *Treatise* 1.3.14. They are the subjects of Chapter 6.

Hume also briefly summarizes all of his contributions to the causation debate as the "one simple argument" he traces through in the *Abstract* (Abstract Preface 4). Although his argument is hardly "simple," both what Hume is saying and whether it is correct was a subject of controversy in his day, and remains a topic of great interest in ours.

In raising "sceptical doubts" about the basis or foundation in reason of our inferences from the observed to the unobserved, and from past and present to the future, Hume is posing for the first time what we now call *the problem of induction*. His argument is so familiar that the problem is often simply called "Hume's Problem." His conclusion in the critical phase of his account of causal inference is dramatic—and entirely negative. Our causal inferences, he concludes, are "are *not* founded on reasoning, or any process of the understanding" (EHU 4.2.15). With this sweeping challenge to virtually every modern philosopher, it is no surprise that the doubts Hume raises here sufficed to tar him for life with a skeptic's brush.

When he steps into the causation debate, Hume translates the traditional distinction between knowledge (*scientia*) and belief (*opinio*) into the terms of his version of the theory of ideas. He divides "all the objects of human reason or enquiry" into two categories: *relations of ideas* and *matters of fact*. His classification is *exhaustive*—there are no other categories—and *exclusive*—no proposition or statement can be in both categories (EHU 4.1.1).

Propositions concerning *relations of ideas* are intuitively or demonstratively certain. They are known a priori, that is, they are discoverable independently of experience by "the mere operation of thought" (EHU 4.1.1). Their truth, therefore, doesn't depend on anything actually existing anywhere in the universe. The proposition *that the interior angles of a Euclidean triangle sum to 180 degrees* is true whether or not there are any Euclidean triangles to be found in the world. Denying that proposition is a contradiction, just as it is contradictory, and not simply false, to say that $8 \times 7 = 55$.

Hume is very deliberately—and radically—restricting what can count as a proposition concerning the relations of ideas. He believes that the only proper objects of knowledge and demonstration are "the sciences of quantity and number," so only geometry, algebra, and arithmetic qualify. Only in those disciplines are "the component parts" of their ideas "entirely similar." The propositions of geometry, algebra, and arithmetic are all composed of the same basic elements—numbers and geometrical figures. Even so, the relations between figures or numbers become more "intricate and involved" as the figures and numbers become more complex. That is why we cannot know the truth of a proposition like *the square of the hypotenuse of a Euclidean triangle is equal to the squares of the other two sides* "without a train of reasoning and enquiry"—without producing a demonstration (EHU 12.3.27).

In sharp contrast to propositions concerning relations of ideas, the truth of propositions concerning *matters of fact* depends on the way the world is. Their contraries are always possible, and their denials never imply contradictions, so they cannot be established by demonstration. Asserting that *Miami is north of Boston* is false, but not contradictory. We can understand what someone who asserts this is saying, even if we are puzzled about how he could have the facts so wrong.

The distinction between *relations of ideas* and *matters of fact* is often called "Hume's Fork." The term suggests an analogy with the fork in a road that forces you to go one way or the other in order to continue your journey. It is generally used with the negative implication that Hume may be illicitly ruling out meaningful propositions that either do not fit into these two categories or fit into both of them. To defuse this objection, however, it should be enough to remember that Hume's categories are his translations of a classificatory distinction that all of his contemporaries and immediate predecessors accept.

Skeptical doubts

Hume's strategy in the critical phase

In the *Enquiry*, Hume begins his critical discussion of causal inference by reminding us that our senses and memories are the sources of the perceptions that are the basis of our beliefs about our past and present experiences. You see, smell, feel, and taste the apple you are eating now; you remember the look, smell, feel, and taste of the apples you have eaten in the past. All these experiences are part of your mental picture of the world. But your picture of the world would be very impoverished if your beliefs about it were restricted to what your past and present experiences tell you. We greatly expand and extend our picture of the world by using our past and present experiences as the basis for forming other beliefs that take us beyond our senses and memories to things we have not observed. Hume wants to know how we do this:

How do we assure ourselves of any matter of fact that takes
us beyond the evidence of our senses and memories?

Your sister receives a postcard; she believes you are in Turkey.
But why does she believe this? She sees the postcard, identifies
the stamp, the postmark, and your handwriting, and notices that
the picture is of the Blue Mosque in Istanbul. But what does any
of that have to do with her belief that you are in Turkey? She takes
there to be some *connection* between your whereabouts and the
postcard, and *infers* that you sent the postcard from Turkey. In
writing the card and mailing it, she takes you to be the cause of a
series of events; her receipt of the card was the final effect in that
series.

There are many other kinds of cases in which we make inferences from something that is present to our senses and memories
to beliefs about something that is not present to them. Hearing a
distinctive voice assures you that your old friend has finally arrived.
Digging up bullets and arrowheads convinces you that you have
found the site of the Battle of Horseshoe Bend. Smelling smoke and
feeling intense heat prompt you to call the Fire Department.

These cases are significantly different from each other. Hume's
interest is in determining what they have in common. In all of
them, you believe that there is some *connection* between "the present
facts" of sense or memory and what you have inferred from them
(EHU 4.1.4). You *link* what you have observed with what you have not
observed.

Hume describes all these cases as *inferences*. He uses the term
inference to mean any movement of thought that takes us from
impressions or ideas to other ideas. We use the three principles
of association—*resemblance, contiguity*, and *causation*—to make
inferences from impressions or idea to other ideas. *Resemblance*
takes you from a picture of your friend to your idea of her, and
contiguity takes you from your present location to thoughts of
something that happened nearby. *Causation*, however, is the only
one of the three associative principles that can take us beyond the
evidence of our senses and memories to belief in matters of fact
and existence that we have not observed. It is the only principle
that takes us from our past and present experience to beliefs about
our future experience. Hume concludes that all these beliefs must
be founded on the relation of *cause and effect*.

Hume's preliminary remarks enable him to answer his initial question of how we assure ourselves of any matters of fact that go beyond the evidence of our senses and memories. We do so by making causal inferences. But answering this question just raises another:

What is the foundation of our inferences concerning cause and effect?

This is the state of play when Hume begins to raise his "sceptical doubts" about whether reason or the understanding is capable of playing this foundational role. If we do make these inferences as the result of an activity or exercise of reason, the reasoning involved must concern either *relations of ideas* or *matters of fact*. Hume first considers whether they concern *relations of ideas*. Here his critical focus is on philosophers like Descartes, in the rationalist tradition, who hold that causal inferences are exercises of reason that establish the relation between cause and effect either by intuition or by demonstrative reasoning. He concludes that our causal inferences cannot be concerned with relations of ideas. Then he turns to the other alternative, *matters of fact*, where his criticism is directed toward philosophers like Locke, in the empiricist tradition, who hold the more modest position that causal inferences are due to probable inferences that yield belief rather than knowledge. His verdict here as well is that these inferences are not based on any activity of reason or the understanding.

Relations of ideas

Hume argues that we never arrive at the conclusions of our causal inferences by the a priori reasoning that intuition and demonstration involves. According to him, we only make these inferences when we have found that instances of one kind of object are constantly conjoined with those of another kind. After you have had numerous experiences of having your headaches relieved after taking aspirin, you *expect* that the aspirin you have just taken will soon relieve your headache. If there is reasoning involved in these inferences, Hume maintains, it cannot be reasoning concerning relations of ideas.

It is important to realize that Hume is telegraphing his constructive views about causal inference as he criticizes the views of the rationalists. To show that our causal beliefs arise from our experience of the constant conjunction of particular objects rather than from a priori reasoning, he offers a thought experiment: Suppose you show an object to a person of "ever so strong natural reason and abilities" that is entirely new to her (EHU 4.1.6). She examines the object carefully and accurately, determining its "sensible qualities" from what she sees, hears, smells, and tastes. Hume says she will never be able to discover any of its "secret powers." We do not know what they are, and we have no direct access to them through our senses.

Hume illustrates his thought experiment with the case of the biblical Adam. Our update of his example provides an effective contemporary take on the point he is making: Imagine that you are brought into the world as an adult, without experience but armed with the intellectual firepower of a Newton or an Einstein. Could you, simply by examining an aspirin tablet's "sensible qualities," determine its "secret power"—that it will relieve your headache?

Hume thinks that we will all freely admit that, when confronted with a completely alien object, we cannot discover its causes and effects by using our reason alone. Since it is like nothing we have ever seen before, we realize that we have no clue what it might do or produce. Few things, of course, are *entirely* alien. Hume reminds us that our experience of similar things provides substantial clues, which we use in ascertaining an object's use or function. Most of our ordinary causal inferences concern things with which we are very familiar. We have made similar judgments about similar things so many times before that we forget we are relying on our past experience. When you see an aspirin, you think "headache relief" so immediately that it seems to be something you grasp directly by the mere operation of your reason, without any need to appeal to your previous experience. He attributes this tendency to *custom*, which, he believes, disguises the fact that we are actually drawing on our experience in these cases.

Hume observes that custom is also operative in cases where we take ourselves to be inferring the necessary connection between a cause and its effect a priori. The ease of the transition from cause to effect, and our feeling of its inevitability, is due to repeated observations of conjunctions between related events, not to a priori inference. However, he reminds us that the effect is totally different from the cause. It is a distinct event, and consequently can never be discovered in the cause. After taking an aspirin you immediately expect it to relieve your headache, but the relief is an entirely distinct event from taking the aspirin. Any connection that you believe holds between them was not established by a priori reasoning, but by experience.

The upshot of all this, Hume says, is that contrary to what the rationalists hold, the ideas of effects are not contained in the ideas of their causes, as they would have to be if our causal inferences were a matter of the relations of ideas. From the point of view of reason alone, for any particular effect that is supposed to be contained in or necessarily connected with a cause, there are many other possible events that can be just as consistently conjoined with the cause. Even if you somehow manage to think that you have connected your ideas of taking aspirin and headache relief prior to experience, there is no contradiction involved in your conceiving that instead of getting relief, your headache will intensify after you take the aspirin, or that you will break out into uncontrollable laughter. Considered independently of experience, these outcomes—along with many others—are equally conceivable, and each possible outcome has an equal claim to being connected with your taking the aspirin. Considered a priori—from the point of view of reason alone—it is completely arbitrary to prefer one outcome to the other. Hume thinks the only way we can avoid this inevitable arbitrariness and actually infer any relation between cause and effect is by accepting "the assistance of experience and observation" (EHU 4.1.11).

If we agree with Hume that our causal beliefs depend on experience, then we can see what has gone wrong when philosophers claim to discover the "ultimate springs and principles" of the universe or to show how power works to produce an effect. All that "the utmost effort of human reason" can do is to rely on experience, observation, and analogy to reduce the number of principles that account for natural phenomena, to simplify those principles, and to explain a number of distinct particulars by reference to a few general causes. We cannot go beyond the bounds of sense to find "ultimate principles" that underlie these causal relations and explanatory principles (EHU 4.1.12).

Hume's conclusions might appear to ignore the dramatic strides that natural philosophers have made by using mathematical principles in their work. Surely, he imagines someone objecting, making physics mathematical makes it an a priori discipline! He responds that pure mathematics is indeed an a priori discipline, which deals exclusively with relations of ideas. But when we apply mathematics in the development of a physical theory, any result begins with, and is ultimately dependent upon, the results of experiment and observation. An astronomer may use mathematical calculations to determine the orbit of a planet, but he bases his calculations on observations that record the planet's location at various times. "Mixed mathematics" may make the astronomer's results more precise, but it does not make them any less dependent on experience. Mathematics may help us draw exact consequences from the laws of nature, but our discovery of the laws themselves is due to experience, and "all the abstract reasonings in the world could never lead us one step" towards discovering these laws (EHU 4.1.13).

When we reason a priori, we consider the idea of the object we regard as a cause independently of any observations we have made or might make of it. We consider it simply as that idea appears to our minds. When we consider the idea this way, it cannot include the idea of any other *distinct* object, including the object we take to be its usual effect. But if considering the idea this way cannot include the effect, then it cannot show us any "inseparable and inviolable connection"—any *necessary connection*—between these ideas (EHU 4.1.13). Trying to reason a priori from your idea of an aspirin tablet, without including any information you might have of its effects from your experiences with aspirin, yields only the simple ideas that compose your complex idea of the aspirin's "sensible qualities." It provides no ideas of its "secret powers"—of its usual effects. Hume concludes that a priori reasoning cannot be the source of the connection between our ideas of a cause and its effect. Contrary to what the majority of his contemporaries and immediate predecessors thought, our causal inferences do not concern relations of ideas.

Matters of fact

Hume now moves to the only possibility remaining on the table. If our causal inferences are the result of an activity of reason or the understanding, then that reasoning must concern *matters of fact.* His discussion of the relations of ideas revealed that our causal inferences are based on *experience*, which gives us an answer to his question about the foundation of our causal inferences. At the same time it raises this further question:

What is the foundation of our conclusions from experience?

Hume suggests that answering this question may prove to be more difficult than anything we encountered in our consideration of the relations of ideas. The argument involved in answering it will be more complicated, and he anticipates that what he says will be met with resistance. He advises us to proceed modestly, making "a kind of merit of our very ignorance" (EHU 4.2.14).

Toward this end, Hume says that he is going to undertake "an easy task" in this section. He will only give us a *negative answer* to his question. This is what he should be doing, given that this is the *critical phase* of his discussion of causal inference. He tells us upfront what his answer will be before he gives us his argument:

> even after we have experience of the operations of cause and effect, our conclusions from that experience are *not* founded on reasoning, or any process of the understanding. (EHU 4.2.15)

Because everyone thinks that these conclusions are based on reason, Hume is very much aware that his radical claim requires a thorough explanation and defense.

He begins by reminding us that his discussion of the relations of ideas has already shown that we have no direct access to the "natural powers and principles"—to the "secret powers"—of bodies. What we do know about them consists only of the surface information our senses provide about their sensible qualities. He considers again the suggestion that if we had access to a body's "secret powers," we would be able to immediately apprehend that a given effect was contained in a certain cause, and we could then infer a priori that a necessary connection obtained between that cause and its effects. But since it is generally agreed that there is "no known connection" between the sensible qualities of an object and its secret powers, Hume maintains that we do not know any of this (EHU 4.2.16).

Even after you have had lots of experience of having your headaches relieved by taking aspirin, so that you believe that taking aspirin will cure the headache you are having now, your inference is still based on the superficial sensible qualities of the aspirin, even if you also assume that the aspirin has "secret powers" that are doing the heavy lifting in relieving your headache. Since these "secret powers" are unknown, they cannot be the basis of your inference. Nonetheless, Hume claims that

> we always presume, when we see like sensible qualities, that they have like secret powers, and expect that effects, similar to those we have experienced, will follow from them. (EHU 4.2.16)

Whenever you see an aspirin tablet that appears similar to others you have taken in the past, you expect that it will relieve your headache, just as the others did.

As we saw in the last section, since we neither intuit nor infer a priori that similar objects have similar secret powers, our presumption must be based in some way on our experience. It also involves some process of the mind or thought. Hume says that he "would willingly know the foundation" of what that process of the mind or thought is (EHU 4.2.16).

Past experience is obviously relevant to both our presumption and the process of thought involved. But our past experience only gives us information about the objects we have actually experienced, as they were at the time we experienced them. Our present experience only gives us information about objects we are experiencing now. Our causal inferences, however, do not just *record* our past and present experiences. They *extend* what we have gathered from these past and present experiences to other objects in the future. Since it is not necessarily true that an object with the same sensible qualities will have the same secret powers that past objects with those sensible qualities had, how do we project these experiences into the future, to other objects that may only appear to be similar to those we have previously experienced? "This is the main question," Hume says, "on which I would insist" (EHU 4.2.16).

He thinks that we can get a handle on this question by considering two propositions, which are clearly different:

(1) You have found that taking aspirin has always been followed by headache relief;

and

(2) Taking aspirin similar to the ones you have taken in the past will relieve the headache you are now experiencing.

There is no question that we do infer propositions like (2) from propositions like (1). But since (1) and (2) are clearly different, if the inference is due to reason, what chain of reasoning takes us from (1) to (2), given that their connection is obviously not *intuitive?*

Hume says that we must acknowledge that in going from (1) to (2), "there is a certain step taken; a process of thought, and an inference, which wants to be explained." He is willing to allow that "the one proposition may be justly inferred from the other," and that "it always is inferred." If we insist that we make the inference by "a chain of reasoning," Hume challenges us to produce that reasoning (EHU 4.2.16).

(1) summarizes my past experience, while (2) makes a prediction about what will happen in my immediate future. To go from (1) to (2), we need some proposition or propositions that will establish an appropriate link between past and future. We need some *connecting principle* that will allow us to construct a chain of reasoning that will take us from (1) to (2). Our reasoning from (1) to (2) using a connecting principle must be either *demonstrative*, concerning relations between the ideas involved, or *probable*, concerning matters of fact and existence.

Hume thinks it is evident that no demonstrative reasoning can bridge the gap between (1) and (2). We can easily conceive of (1) being true while (2) is false. One way of seeing this is by conceiving that the fact that the course of nature may change does not involve a contradiction. In such a case, objects seemingly similar to those we have experienced in the past may have very different effects in the future. The tomatoes from your garden have always been tasty, so you expect that the ones you pick next week will be tasty as well. But you can easily conceive of them tasting sour instead, and it is possible that they might be sour. For all you know, the change might be due to the effects of acid rain, which in Hume's terms would count as a change in the course of nature. But since we can intelligibly conceive of this change in the course of nature, he holds that such a change implies no contradiction, which means that it cannot be shown to be false by any demonstrative argument or abstract a priori reasoning. He concludes that demonstrative reasoning cannot provide the chain of reasoning that we need to take us from (1) to (2).

If reason or the understanding is to be the basis of an inference from (1) to (2), then the reasoning involved must be *probable reasoning*—the only form of reasoning left. But Hume thinks that there is no probable argument that can provide a just inference from past to future. Any attempt to infer (2) from (1) by a probable inference will be viciously circular—it will involve supposing what we are trying to prove.

Hume spells out the circularity this way. Any reasoning from experience that takes us from (1) to (2) must employ some *connecting principle*—some principle that connects the past with the future. Since one thing that keeps us from moving directly from past to future is the possibility that the course of nature might change, it seems plausible to think that the connecting principle we need must assure us that the course of nature will not change. So when you infer that the aspirin you are about to take will relieve your headache, if your inference is determined by reasoning, that reasoning must be based upon the principle that nature is uniform over time. That means we need something like this principle, which we will call the *Uniformity Principle*, or [UP] for short:

[UP] The future will be like the past

Adopting [UP] will indeed allow us to go from statements about past experience to statements about the future. But it states a matter of fact, not a relation of ideas. Before it can be used to establish that our causal inferences are determined by reason, we need to ask about our basis for adopting it. [UP] clearly is not *intuitive*, nor is it *demonstrative*, as we see from the arguments Hume has already considered; so, as he points out, only probable arguments could establish it. But that would be to try to establish probable arguments by an argument using probable arguments, which would eventually include [UP] itself. As Hume rightly concludes, that would be viciously circular. Probable inference cannot under-write our inferences from past to future, so our causal inferences are not based on any activity of reason or the understanding.

This concludes Hume's main line of argument for the critical aspect of his treatment of causal inference. Before closing, however, he supplements his main argument with a corollary that deals with one way in which holdouts might try to defend the view that our causal inferences are based on reason. He considers someone who suggests that after a number of uniform experiences, we rationally infer a connection between an object's sensible qualities and its secret powers. It is tempting to think that after you have had enough experience of taking aspirin and headache relief, you can conclude that there is a connection between the sensible qualities—its color, shape, smell, and taste—of aspirin and its secret power to relieve headaches. But he points out that this just raises the same question we have been considering in a slightly different form. For your inference to be based on reason, you still need some *connecting principle* to take you from your past conclu-sions about the relations between aspirin's sensible qualities and its secret powers to your projection that the aspirin you are about to take, which admittedly has quite similar sensible qualities, will also have the secret power to relieve your headache. This connecting principle will be equivalent to the Uniformity Principle [UP], and so will suffer the same fate.

Hume's arguments have exhausted the ways reason might establish a connection between cause and effect to show that our causal inferences are based on reason. He cautions us that he offers his "sceptical doubts" not as a "discouragement, but rather an incitement … to attempt something more full and satisfactory" (EHU 4.1.3). Having cleared the way for the constructive aspect of his account, Hume is ready to do just that.

5

Causal inference: a skeptical solution

Hume's constructive account of causal inference is contained in Section 5 of the first *Enquiry* and in Sections 7–10 of Book I of the *Treatise*. His abbreviated discussion in the *Abstract* is very close to the *Enquiry* version. As we did with the critical aspect of his account, we follow the *Enquiry* version, supplementing it occasionally with points he makes in the *Treatise* and *Abstract*.

The *critical phase* of Hume's discussion of causal inference raises "sceptical doubts about the operations of the understanding." He doubts whether our causal inferences are due to the exercise of reason. Hume calls the *constructive phase* of his discussion "a sceptical solution of these doubts," but he does not explain what he means by this phrase. What is a "sceptical solution"?

The best way to understand what Hume means is to contrast a *skeptical solution* with what we might call a *straight solution* to his skeptical doubts. A straight solution would be an attempt to show that, contrary to what he has argued, our causal inferences are based on reason. Anyone offering such a response must either show that Hume's arguments for his skeptical doubts are flawed in some specific way, or present an alternative foundation in reason that his arguments do not cover.

The prospects for a straight solution are not good. Hume's arguments do not contain any obvious flaws, and any attempt to provide an alternative foundation in reason would have to be more

complex than the arguments that he has criticized. But such sophis-
ticated forms of reasoning are not—and in many cases cannot
be—used by many ordinary people, young children, and even
animals. Yet we know that they make inferences that go beyond
their senses and memories, and that their ability to make casual
inferences improves with experience, so any attempt to get around
Hume's arguments in this way will also fail.

Since we routinely make causal inferences, we need to account
for how we make them in a way that does not encourage the
"pretence of reason" that straight solutions exemplify (EHU 5.1.1).
In contrast with straight solutions, Hume's *skeptical solution* aims
to determine the principles of human nature that are the basis
of our causal inferences, while acknowledging that in our inferences from experience we take a step that is not supported by any
argument or process of reason. But

> if the mind be not engaged by argument to make this step, it
> must be induced by some other principle of equal weight and
> authority; and that principle will preserve its influence as long
> as human nature remains the same. (EHU 5.1.2)

His skeptical solution proceeds on the premise that it is "worth the
pains of enquiry" to determine just what principle of human nature
is responsible for our making this step, and so is also responsible
for our causal inferences (EHU 5.1.2).

Hume begins by backtracking a bit. He reminds us of the thought
experiment he asked us to perform in the previous section. Suppose
you were brought suddenly into the world as an adult, armed
with all the intellectual firepower of a Newton or an Einstein, but
completely without experience. You could observe a continual
succession of objects, but you would not be able to conclude, either
by inspecting them or by reasoning about them, that any of them
were causally related. For all your ability to reason, you would not
be able to go beyond your senses and memories.

Now suppose you have lived in the world a while, and have
accumulated considerably more experience. You begin to notice
that similar objects or events are constantly conjoined with one
another. You also find that when an event of one kind has been
constantly conjoined with events of another kind, you cannot help
but *expect* an event of the other kind to occur. After you have

frequently experienced smoke and fire together, when you see smoke, you expect that fire is in the vicinity. You are *inferring* that there is a fire in the vicinity from the appearance of the smoke.

All you have experienced are the constant conjunctions of events of those kinds. You know nothing about what "secret powers" events of either type may or may not have. You know nothing about how fire *produces* smoke. No process of reasoning leads you to expect that you will soon see fire when you see smoke. But you are still determined—and here Hume means *caused*—to make the inference from smoke to fire. So there must be some other principle that leads you to draw this conclusion.

Custom and habit

Hume maintains that this principle is *custom* or *habit*:

> wherever the repetition of any particular act or operation produces a propensity to renew the same act or operation, without being impelled by any reasoning or process of the understanding, we always say, that this propensity is the effect of *Custom*. (EHU 5.1.5)

Repeated experiences of smoke and fire create a "propensity"—a tendency—in your mind to expect the one whenever you experience the other. This propensity is the effect of the customary association of the ideas of smoke and fire in your experience. *Custom* or *habit*, then, is the "principle of equal weight and authority" that determines—causes—you to expect fire where there is smoke. This principle is at the heart of Hume's *skeptical solution*.

Even though we have located the principle, it is important to see that this is not a *new* principle by which our minds operate. Hume describes the operation of the principle as a causal process: custom or habit is the cause of the particular propensity that you form after your repeated experiences of the constant conjunction of smoke and fire. We know from our earlier discussion of Hume's mental machinery that causation is one of the principles of association; in fact, it is the only one of those principles that is capable of taking us beyond our senses and memories. *Custom or habit* is just another name for *association*.

Hume could be confident that his readers would understand that he is using *custom* and *habit* to refer to the associative principles. In his chapter "Of the Association of Ideas" in *An Essay concerning Human Understanding*, Locke describes the association of ideas using the terms custom and habit, as he does when he says that "custom settles habits of thinking in the understanding" (Essay 2.33.6). Hume is following Locke in using this terminology, but their views about the nature of association could not be more different. Locke thought the association of ideas was a "disease of the mind" that amounted to a form of "*Madness*," an irrational and unnatural connecting of ideas that are not logically connected (Essay 2.33.4). His examples include the case of a person who could not go into the room where a loved one died because of the associations the room held for him. Another is a case where a child's aversion to a particular book is due to his associating it with the pain he suffered when his teacher harshly corrected him for misunderstanding it. Hume, on the other hand, regards association as the natural process that produces *all* our inferences that go beyond immediate experience and memory.

In keeping with his project of providing a naturalistic account of how our minds work, Hume is giving an empirical explanation of our propensity to make causal inferences. He appeals to "a principle of human nature, which is universally acknowledged, and which is well known by its effects" (EHU 5.1.5). His skeptical solution—his constructive account of our causal inferences—is radical in three significant ways: He rejects reason as the basis for our inferences; he substitutes a principle that Locke likened to madness as their basis; and in doing so, he provides a causal account of our causal inferences.

For additional confirmation of his position, Hume calls attention to the fact that we are frequently able to draw an inference from many cases that we cannot draw from a single case, even though the single case is no different from the other cases. A single egg will not allow us to tell whether future eggs will be tasty or not, while after we have lots of experience with eggs, we can distinguish a rotten egg from a good one. Association provides the only intelligible explanation of this phenomenon. Reason alone cannot glean any more useful information from repeated experiences of many eggs than it can from the examination of a single case. We must, therefore, be "determined by CUSTOM alone" to make these judgments (Abstract 15).

Hume concludes that custom operates "by making us expect for the future, a similar train of events with those which have appeared in the past" (EHU 5.1.6). It determines us, "in all instances, to suppose the future conformable to the past." Custom thus turns out to be the source of what, in the previous chapter, we called the *Uniformity Principle*—the belief that the future will be like the past. "However easy this step may seem, reason would never, to all eternity, be able to make it" (Abstract 16).

Custom, not reason, makes experience *useful*. It teaches us how to determine the means to our ends, and how to use our natural powers to make things happen. If it were not for custom, we would not be able to act, much less *explain* our actions. This is in itself a remarkable discovery. But as Hume stresses, it "leads us to others, that are still more curious" (Abstract 17).

Belief

Hume has been focusing on the role of experienced constant conjunctions in producing our causal inferences. But now he turns to another feature of those inferences. When we infer an effect from a cause, we *expect* that the effect will occur, which is more than just *conceiving* that it will occur. Expectations are not mere conceptions; they are *beliefs*. When I expect that the aspirin I just took will relieve my headache, I am not abstractly conceiving of headache relief: I believe that the aspirin will actually relieve it. What is the difference between conceiving of headache relief and believing that the aspirin I took will relieve my headache?

Hume notices that one important difference between believing and conceiving is that for belief, there must be some object present to the memory or senses in addition to the customary conjunctions. This is not necessary for mere conception. I must be aware that I have actually taken an aspirin if I am to believe that it will relieve my headache, but I can conceive of headache relief under any circumstances whatsoever.

Hume concludes that after we have experienced a customary conjunction between one type of object and another, when we are presented with an object of one type, our belief that we will soon experience an object of the other type "is the necessary result" of our present experience. In these circumstances, belief is as unavoidable as feeling affection in the presence of a close friend, or anger and fear when someone threatens us. For Hume, "all these operations are a species of natural instincts, which no reasoning or process of the thought and understanding is able either to produce or to prevent" (EHU 5.1.8).

This is another remarkable result. Many philosophers in the modern period, including Descartes, not only thought that causal beliefs were products of an exercise of reason, they also thought that belief was the product of a *simple act of thought*—the voluntary choice of a free will. If Hume is right, this traditional picture of belief formation is completely wrong. Belief formation is not a matter of choice.

Hume is aware how radical his account of belief is, and he is very proud of it. He thinks that no previous philosopher has provided an adequate account of belief. Philosophers have not asked the right questions about the nature of belief, or asked how we form them. He proposes to continue his inquiry into the nature of belief by asking in another way what distinguishes a belief from a conception or fiction. Since we have the ability to form almost any possible complex idea by separating and combining our ideas, what is the difference between ideas created in this way, which are purely *fictitious*, and *beliefs*?

Hume argues that the difference between a fictitious creation of my imagination and a belief cannot be that there is some further idea that beliefs have and fictions lack. If there were some such idea, all we would have to do is to take that idea and add it to any conception whatsoever, which would turn that conception into a belief. Suppose you believe that there are horses, but you do not believe that there are unicorns, even though you have a clear conception of what unicorns are like. If there were some particular idea that made your idea of horses a belief, you could separate that idea from your idea of horses and attach it to your idea of unicorns. You would then believe that there are unicorns. Since you could attach the idea to any other idea, you would be free to believe absolutely anything you like. Since we are not free to believe anything we like, the difference between belief and fiction cannot be that some additional idea is attached to beliefs and not to fictions.

Hume concludes that the difference between fiction and belief must consist in some particular *way* or *manner* of conceiving an idea. It must be some *sentiment*—some *feeling*—that beliefs have and fictions do not have. This sentiment or feeling must be aroused in us, as are all sentiments or feelings, "by nature"—by the operation of the associative principles. It also must be excited in us in virtue of the particular situation in which we find ourselves. Hume explains:

> Whenever any object is presented to the memory or senses, it immediately, by the force of custom, carries the imagination to conceive that object, which is usually conjoined to it; and this conception is attended with a feeling or sentiment, different from the loose reveries of the fancy. In this consists the whole nature of belief. (EHU 5.2.11)

After we have repeated experience of two sorts of objects constantly conjoined, when we are presented with one of them, our mind is led to conceive of the associated object in a particular manner—with a particular feeling—that distinguishes it from fictions.

Hume is aware that recognizing this sentiment is one thing, but defining it is another, just as it is difficult, if not impossible, to define what cold or anger feels like to someone who has never had those particular feelings. Even though we may not be able to define this particular feeling, we can describe it, if only by analogy. He begins by using terms like *vivid* and *lively*, which seem to imply that the distinction is just one of degree of intensity of feeling. But he believes that there are also other differences between fictions and beliefs. Beliefs are a more forceful, firm, steady conception of an object than any of the fictions of the imagination. Beliefs also receive more consideration in our thoughts, and have more weight and importance in our deliberations. Beliefs have a greater influence on our passions, and they influence our actions. While Hume was never entirely satisfied with his attempts to characterize the feeling or sentiment that distinguishes beliefs from conceptions, it is important to notice that his descriptions go far beyond the mere notion of intensity of feeling that his initial terms encourage.

By this point, Hume has determined that it is the particular "*manner* of conception"—the feelings of force and vivacity with which the idea is conceived—that distinguishes a belief from a mere conception (EHU 5.2.12). We are much clearer about the nature of belief and the circumstances under which we form beliefs. But there is one important question about belief formation that he has not yet addressed: In a causal inference, how does the idea of the effect *acquire* enough force and vivacity for it to qualify as a belief and not just a conception?

Hume approaches this question in what might seem to be a roundabout manner. Given what we have learned about belief formation and causal inference, he thinks that it will not be difficult to find other mental operations that are analogous. Once we find them, he predicts that we can "trace up these phenomena to principles still more general" (EHU 5.2.13). Hume is proceeding like a good Newtonian. He wants to simplify his account of how our minds work by explaining a variety of phenomena with a few general principles.

The phenomena Hume investigates are the two other associative principles: *resemblance* and *contiguity*. They too establish connections among certain of our ideas, and unite our thoughts "by a gentle and insensible movement." His strategy is to integrate his treatment of causal belief with a general account of the workings of the associative principles. He proceeds by asking this question: whenever one of the associative principles takes us from an object presented to our senses or memories to a conception of another object that is correlated with it in our experience, do we always reach a steadier and stronger conception of that object than we would have otherwise? Since this is the case with the relation of cause and effect, if it is also the case with resemblance and contiguity, we can establish it "as a general law, which takes place in all the operations of the mind" (EHU 5.2.14).

Hume believes that determining whether or not resemblance and contiguity also produce stronger and steadier conceptions of their objects will not only integrate his account of the workings of the associative principles, it will also answer his question about how the idea of the effect becomes a belief in causal inferences. When we see how resemblance and contiguity operate, we will be able to see that causation works in the same way.

Resemblance clearly produces stronger and steadier conceptions of its objects. Suppose your close friend, who has been traveling in Europe all summer, emails you a picture that shows her delight at visiting the Acropolis in Athens. Your idea of her, which has become somewhat less vivid in her long absence, is enlivened considerably by the resemblance between your friend and her picture, as are your feelings for her. If the picture included the Acropolis but not your friend, none of this would have happened, because the associative principle of resemblance would not be operative. But how did the picture enliven your idea of your friend? Hume reminds us that our impressions of her image in the picture were as forceful and vivid as any impressions. Some of their force and vivacity gets transferred across the resemblance relation to your idea of your friend, which made your idea more vivid than it was before you received her picture.

Turning then to the effects of *contiguity*, Hume observes that distance diminishes the force of any idea. The closer we come to an object in time and space, even though we may not be close enough to have a present impression of it, the more it affects our minds, so that our idea of it begins to increase in force and vivacity until its force and vivacity is close to that of a present impression. Events that happen in your hometown make more of an impression on you when you are living there than when you have been away for several years and read about them on the internet. Even though your ideas of home, given a long absence, are not as vivid as they would be if you were actually there, they are still aroused by news of home, and you identify with your hometown in a way that you would not identify with news of some place where you have never lived or even visited.

Contiguity in place enlivens ideas even when they are not contiguous in time. Visiting the site of Troy makes your ideas of the Trojan Wars and its heroes more vivid than they were before, when all you knew about Troy was from what you had read about it. The force and vivacity of your impressions of the site transfer across the contiguity relation to your idea of Troy, enlivening it.

Although we have already seen the effects of *causation* in the production of belief, Hume cannot resist reinforcing the parallels he has just drawn with resemblance and contiguity by offering an example where causation works in a similar way. When we meet the daughter of a long-dead friend whom we loved and admired, her presence "instantly" revives our idea of her mother. We recall our memories of her "in more lively colours than they would otherwise have appeared to us" if we had not met her daughter (EHU 5.2.19).

All of these cases presuppose our belief in the person or object that is correlated with our present impressions; otherwise, the relation would have no effect. Our present impressions, which are forceful and vivid, transfer some of their force and vivacity to our idea of the person or object, raising its level of force and vivacity almost to the level of our present impressions.

Hume thinks that this is

> the whole operation of the mind, in all our conclusions concerning matter of fact and existence; and it is a satisfaction to find some analogies, by which it may be explained. The transition from a present object does in all cases give strength and solidity to the related ideas. (EHU 5.2.20)

Hume can now explain how an idea comes to be conceived in such a manner that it constitutes a belief. As I become accustomed to aspirin's relieving my headaches, I develop a propensity—a tendency—to expect headache relief to follow my taking aspirin. That propensity is due to the associative bond that my repeated experiences of taking aspirin followed by headache relief have formed. My present impressions of taking an aspirin are as forceful and vivid as anything could be. Some of their force and vivacity transfer through the associative path to the idea of headache relief, enlivening it with enough force and vivacity to give it the "strength and solidity" that constitutes belief. As we will see in Chapter 9, he uses the idea that the associative principles transmit force and vivacity from an impression to an idea in his explanation of sympathy and the moral sentiments. Hume has achieved both his aims: he has integrated his account of how the associative principles operate, and he has answered his final question about belief and causal inference.

Since I do not know how aspirin relieves headaches, Hume emphasizes that it is fortunate that there is "a kind of pre-established harmony between the course of nature and the succession of our ideas" that teaches me to take an aspirin whenever I have a headache. In some remarkably proto-Darwinian language, he describes the work of the principles of association as "necessary to the subsistence of our species, and the regulation of our conduct, in every circumstance and occurrence of human life" (EHU 5.2.21). If custom did not operate this way, he maintains, we would have been limited to the narrow sphere of our present impressions and memories, and would never have been able to adjust means to ends or to use our natural powers to produce good and avoid evil. Simply put, without the operations of custom we would not know how to navigate in the world.

Given how essential the ability to make causal inferences is "to the subsistence of all human creatures," it is fortunate that nature has not trusted it to "the fallacious deductions of our reason." At its best, it works very slowly and is always liable to error and mistake. It is far better that "the ordinary wisdom of nature" has established this necessary process of thought as an instinct or mechanical tendency (EHU 5.2.22).

Hume's constructive account of causal inference is now complete. The only task remaining is to account for our idea of the necessary connection that is involved in our idea of causation. We will examine his treatment of that idea in the next chapter.

6

The idea of necessary connection

Hume's discussion of our idea of necessary connection is the final component of his contribution to the early modern causation debate. Every modern philosopher, Hume included, agrees that our idea of causation involves the idea of a *necessary connection* between a cause and its effect. A cause *must* produce its effect. They differ, however, about how to understand the nature of that connection.

Hume anticipates someone asking why he chose to discuss causal inference without first determining the nature of the causal relation itself. In the *Treatise*, he responds to this objection by saying that he would have done so if he could have, but it was not possible, because "the nature of the relation depends so much on the inference." Our idea of the necessary connection between a cause and its effect depends on the nature of our causal inferences, and not the other way round, as many thought. Hume tells us that when he realized the direction of the dependence, he was obliged instead to proceed in "this seemingly preposterous manner," making use of terms before he could define them precisely. He promises to "correct this fault" with his account of our idea of necessary connection, by giving us a "precise definition of cause and effect" (T 1.3.14.29). That is exactly what he does. His definition of our idea of causation completes his discussion of necessary connection.

Hume's treatments of our idea of necessary connection in Section 7 of the first *Enquiry* and in *Treatise* 1.3.14 closely parallel one another. There is also a very brief summary of this part of his argument in the *Abstract*. Our account here draws from both the *Enquiry* and the *Treatise*. The most substantial difference between the two accounts is in their definitions of *cause*. In addition to differing in some matters of detail, the *Treatise* defines our idea of cause in terms of philosophical and natural relations (see Chapter 3), whereas Hume drops this terminology entirely in the *Enquiry*. For that part of our discussion, we follow the *Enquiry*, which more straightforwardly applies Hume's account of definition in determining the content of our idea of causation.

Although the idea of necessary connection was the *primary* concept the moderns used in their attempts to capture the relation between cause and effect, it was not the *only* one. The causation debate actually revolved around a family of key terms, among them *efficacy*, *agency*, *power*, *force*, *energy*, and *productive quality*. Hume believes that these notions form a kind of definitional circle. Although each term can be defined using one or more of the other terms in the circle, the defining terms are no clearer than the original. Since they are "all nearly synonimous," Hume maintains that it is "an absurdity to employ any of them in defining the rest." If someone tries to define *cause*, for instance, *as having a quality that is productive of another*, he will not be saying anything:

> For what does he mean by *production*? Can he give any definition of it, that will not be the same with that of causation? If he can; I desire it may be produced. If he cannot; he here runs in a circle, and gives a synonimous term instead of a definition. (T 1.3.2.10)

Since Hume regards the various terms philosophers have used to characterize the necessity of the relation between a cause and its effect as synonyms, he treats them as such throughout his account. Most of his discussion concerns *power* or *necessary connection*, which he considers tantamount to one idea. When he focuses on one of these two terms, what he concludes about it applies to the other as well. He sometimes throws other terms from the definitional circle into the mix, especially *energy* and *force*, but since they are synonyms as well, he is not changing the subject when he does this.

Hume is convinced that "there are no ideas, which occur in metaphysics, more obscure and uncertain" than the terms in this definitional circle. It is impossible to get clear about the content of our idea of causation without dealing with *necessary connection*, *power*, and the other terms in the circle first. Hume's objective, therefore, is "to fix ... the precise meaning of these terms, and thereby remove some part of that obscurity, which is so much complained of in this species of philosophy" (EHU 7.1.3). Because these terms have currency in the theories of his immediate predecessors and contemporaries, he cannot just move straight to the constructive work of determining their precise meaning. He must first show what is wrong with the leading views about them. Like his treatment of causal inference, then, his task here has both *critical* and *constructive* aspects. It provides another excellent illustration of his project and method at work. As he proceeds, we will see that he often brings in points with which we are familiar from both his critical and constructive accounts of causal inference.

Necessary connection: critical phase

In the *Enquiry*, Hume begins with a review of his account of definition, which we discussed in Chapter 3, since he uses it here to deliver the most dramatic result we have seen thus far. He reminds us that the chief obstacles to making substantial improvements in philosophy are that the ideas we use are obscure, and our terms are ambiguous. To make progress, we need to quit pretending to get clear about our terms by defining them in terms of other equally ambiguous terms. We need to get to "the true and real subject of the controversy"—the ideas involved, and determine their exact content (EHU 8.1.1). Hume believes his account of definition will allow him to do just that.

Recall that Hume's account of definition, which is essentially the *reverse* of the Copy Principle, uses a simple series of tests to determine the meaning or cognitive content of a term or idea. Here is how it works: Begin with a term. Ask what idea is annexed to it. If there is no such idea, then the term has no cognitive content, however prominently it figures in philosophy or theology. If there is an idea annexed to the term, and it is complex, break it up into the simple ideas that compose it. Then trace each component simple idea back to the impressions that gave rise to it. If the process fails at any point, the idea in question lacks cognitive content. When carried through successfully, however, the theory yields a "just definition"—a precise account of the content of the troublesome idea or term (EHU 7.2.29).

To get clear about philosophically contentious ideas like power or necessary connection, Hume's account of definition directs us to look for impressions in all the possible sources from which we might derive them. There are two sources: *external impressions* of our "*outward* senses"—the impressions we get from our five senses, and *internal impressions* of "sentiment or *inward* impression"— impressions we get of the activities and operations of our own minds (EHU 7.1.6). Hume finds, in the work of his predecessors, three leading contenders for the sources in impressions from which our idea of power or necessary connection might be derived.

The first contender is that we get an idea of power from our *external impressions* of the interactions of physical objects. Locke thought that when we see a billiard ball moving another by impulse, the transfer of its motion to the other ball is enough to give us an idea of power. But the first ball did not originate its own motion. It was only moving because something else moved it. So the idea of power we get from a case like this is only a *secondary* idea of power, which Locke calls *passive power*.

The *primary* idea of power, which Locke calls *active power*, is the second contender for the source of our idea of power. The first ball in our previous example was set in motion by Samantha's cue, after she set up the shot and decided to make it. In making decisions like this to move our bodies, Locke thought that we have immediate and direct *internal impressions* of the active power of our wills to move our bodies. Locke also thought that we also have direct evidence from internal impressions of the power of our wills when we choose to call up or dismiss ideas.

The third contender Hume considers for the source of our idea of power or necessary connection is *occasionalism*, a view that was prominent in the rationalist tradition, especially among Cartesians. Descartes himself arguably held a version of this view, but its most prominent defender, and the one whose work Hume knew best, was Nicholas Malebranche. According to Malebranche, God is the only source of power or necessary connection. What we take to be *causes*—either of interactions among physical objects, or of my voluntary bodily movements and consideration of ideas—are really not causes at all. They are only the *occasions* where God makes it the case that one physical object follows another, or where my decision to throw the ball precedes the movements of my arm, or my choice to recall my summer vacation precedes my thoughts of Istanbul.

Hume first argues against Locke's proposal that we can get an idea of power by observing the interactions of physical objects. He reminds us that, as we saw in his discussion of causal inference, examining single particular cases that we regard as cause and effect never yields any quality that binds or ties the effect to the cause, or makes the effect the infallible consequence of the cause. All we find in a single case is that the object or event that we take to be the effect in fact *follows* the object or event we regard as its cause. This is all that we get from our "outward senses," and we feel no sentiment or internal impression from observing this succession of objects. So the source of our idea of power or necessary connection cannot be a single case of events or objects that we take to be causally related.

When we observe an object for the very first time, we cannot guess what effect might result from it. But if the power or energy of a cause were something that we could discover from the information that our senses give us, we would be able to foresee with certainty what effects it would produce without ever having to experience them. But that never happens. We can determine the sensible qualities of bodies—their solidity, extension, and motion—by observing them, but they never imply any other event that might result from them. They tell us nothing about what power or energy that body might have, so it is impossible that we could derive the idea of power from contemplating bodies in single instances of their operation.

Perhaps the source of our idea of power or necessary connection comes, not from observation of the behavior of bodies, but from reflection on the contents of our own minds, and thus is copied from some *internal impression*. Since Locke thinks that we feel that our wills can command the movement of parts of our bodies, as well as our ability to call up or dismiss our ideas, he would say that we are always conscious of our internal power. Any time I voluntarily choose to move my arms, or to think about my summer vacation, I am aware of the influence of my will. I am therefore certain that I have these powers, as do all other intelligent creatures.

But, Hume asks, what impressions do we really have of the influence of our wills over our bodies? When you are typing, if you choose to continue to type, your fingers continue to move over the keyboard. When you decide to stop, they stop moving. We are all aware that in most ordinary cases, movements of our bodies *follow* our willing that those bodily movements occur. However, the fact that our wills have the influence they do is a matter of fact, just like any other natural event. We learn about the influence our wills have over our bodies from our experiences of willing—from our choices and decisions and the subsequent movements of our bodies. You do not learn about the influence of your will from any internal impression of power or energy that somehow connects your decision to type with the movements of your fingers and makes those movements the infallible consequences of your decision. In addition, although you are aware that your fingers do move over the keyboard after you decide to type, you are totally ignorant of *how* this happens.

Hume reminds us that our ignorance of how our wills move our bodies is not at all surprising, given that we really know nothing about the relations between our minds and our bodies. He thinks that everyone will agree that nothing is more mysterious than the mind–body relation where, according to some philosophers, a supposed spiritual substance is somehow united with, and has control over, a material substance.

Of course, if we did have the kind of internal impression of the power or energy of our wills that those philosophers think we have, we would know the connections between our decisions and our bodily movements. We would also know the "secret union" of mind and body, as well as the natures of both (EHU 7.1.11). Then we would know what makes it possible for our minds to move our bodies. But, Hume says, we know nothing of this.

We also know, he continues, that our wills do not have complete control over the movements of all the parts of our bodies. We cannot move all the parts of our bodies with equal ease, and some parts we cannot move at all, no matter how hard we try. You can wiggle your toes, but you can only wiggle your ears a bit, and with great difficulty, if you can wiggle them at all. Try as you might, you cannot voluntarily move your pancreas without moving the rest of your body. As Hume points out, if you were aware that you had the power to move your fingers but not your pancreas, you would know these things without having ever tried to move either. But you do not know these things. We only learn of the influence of our wills through experience, and experience teaches us only that one event constantly follows the other. It never tells us the "secret connexion" that binds those events together (EHU 7.1.13).

Finally, Hume notes that when we decide to move our arms, we are aware that our wills do not move them *directly*. Our arms' movements are the last link in a long chain of events inside our bodies, involving our brains, central nervous systems, and various muscles and nerves. We do not understand all the details that are involved in this process, and we do not need to understand them in order to move our arms. He thinks this shows that moving our arms is something that is mysterious and unintelligible to us. Our ability to move our arms is not something that we know directly and completely because we are immediately and directly aware of the influence of our wills. If we were aware of the power that makes this chain of events happen, we would be aware of all the physical details the exercise of that power produces. All power is relative to its effect—it is the effect that makes that power the particular power that it is. But then if I cannot know the effect, I cannot know the power either.

Hume concludes that we do not get our idea of power from any internal impressions of our power to voluntarily move our bodies. Although the motions of our bodies follow the commands of our wills, the power by which we bring these movements about is as unknown and inconceivable as it is with any other natural events.

If Locke was wrong in claiming that the connection between our wills and bodily movements is the source of our idea of power, energy, or force, then might he still be right that the source is our immediate awareness of our power to choose whether to consider an idea or to dismiss it? Hume thinks that this prospect is no more promising. Arguments parallel to those we just looked at show that even our experience of considering and dismissing ideas gives us no real idea of power or energy.

Hume argues that to know a power is to know the circumstances in the cause that enables it to produce the effect, because these claims are synonymous. To know a power, we must know the cause, the effect, and the relation between them. But no one claims to know the relation between the nature of our minds and the nature of our ideas, much less our minds' ability to produce ideas at will. Not only do we never feel or know such a power, we cannot even conceive of it. We are only aware of the presence of an idea in our minds when it follows our decision to call up that idea. When you choose to think about the trip you will take to Venice next summer, the idea of Venice comes into your consciousness. But how this comes about—the power that produces your idea—is entirely beyond your comprehension.

Besides, Hume maintains, our command over our ideas is limited, in much the same way as our command over moving the parts of our bodies is limited. We are aware of the limitations of our minds' command over our ideas the same way we learn about the limits of our minds' command over our bodies—through experience and observation. However limited our minds' authority over our ideas may be, it is unquestionably more limited when it comes to our sentiments and passions. We cannot just choose to feel pride or love, and we certainly cannot choose what to believe. We cannot voluntarily dismiss strong feelings of jealousy, envy, or anger. No one believes we can explain why these limits exist, or why we lack the power to consider or dismiss some ideas but not others.

Further, what command we do have over our thoughts varies. When we are ill, tired, or hungry, we have less command over our thoughts than we do when we are healthy, rested, and well fed. We only know about these variations through experience. Philosophers like Locke might argue that they must be due to some "secret mechanism" on which these effects depend. But this mechanism is totally unknown and incomprehensible to us, which makes the power and energy of our wills equally unknown and incomprehensible.

At this point, Hume is satisfied that our ability to call up and dismiss ideas provides no more evidence of power or energy in our wills than does our ability to move our bodies. In neither case did we find the internal impressions that were supposed to be the source of our idea of power. He now moves to the only remaining contender of the candidates for the source of the idea of power or necessary connection—Malebranche's *occasionalism*.

Malebranche agrees with Hume that we cannot find the source of our idea of necessary connection in any of the possibilities he has so far considered. But occasionalists claim that just because the source of the idea of power or necessary connection cannot be found *in* the world, it does not mean that there is no source at all. For occasionalists, the source lies *outside* the world. God is the only being with real power—the only being whose will is the ultimate and original cause of everything. The objects or events that we commonly call *causes* are really nothing but *occasions* where God wills that particular kinds of objects are always conjoined with objects of another kind. When we believe that lightning is the cause of thunder or that smoke is the effect of fire, we are wrong. Particular instances of those phenomena are just *occasions* where God exercises his will that thunder should be conjoined with lightning and smoke with fire.

Hume initially responds that occasionalists unwittingly end up demeaning God when their aim is to glorify him. Surely if God's power were as great as they suppose, he would delegate some of it to his creatures rather than electing to do everything himself. Why did he not have the foresight to organize the world at the time he created it so "that stupendous machine" operates as it should without any need for his continuous tinkering (EHU 7.1.22)?

Hume follows up this facetious response with two more serious arguments designed to show that there is something seriously wrong with occasionalism. First, anyone who is aware of the narrow limits of our minds should suspect that this theory goes beyond the reach of our faculties, since it draws extraordinary conclusions that are remote from our ordinary lives and everyday experience. It goes so far beyond our sphere of experience, in fact, that it takes us into "fairy land," as Hume puts it. In this rarified atmosphere, we have no reason to rely on the analogies, probabilities, and common methods of argument that we use in settling questions about causes and effects (EHU 7.1.24). The occasionalists' appeal to an ultimate reality beyond experience is exactly the kind of appeal to "ultimate original principles" that Hume has argued is unintelligible.

In addition, the occasionalists' argument depends on emphasizing our ignorance of the ways bodies operate on one another, and on the incomprehensibility of their force and energy. But since our only idea of God is based on extrapolating from our own faculties, why is it that our ignorance and limitations do not apply to God as well?

Hume's critical account of our ideas of power and necessary connection has produced negative results. In searching for the impressions that are the source of our ideas of power, necessary connection, and other synonymous terms, we have found that considering single cases of body–body, mind–body, and mind–mind causation gives us no idea of the power by which the cause operates, or of the connection between the cause and its supposed effect. All these cases involve events that we found to be separate and distinct. One event followed another, but there seemed to be no link or tie between them. They were "*conjoined*, but never *connected*" (EHU 7.2.26). Since we cannot have an idea of something that has no source in either outward sense or internal sentiment, the conclusion it *seems* we must draw is that we really have no idea of power or necessary connection, and that therefore these terms are unintelligible, whether they are used in philosophy or in ordinary life.

Necessary connection: constructive phase

Hume, however, is unwilling to draw this pessimistic conclusion. He believes that his predecessors missed a possible source in impressions of that idea. He begins by reminding us of something we noticed more than once in our earlier discussions of the idea of causation. No matter how carefully we examine an object, we find that independently of experience, we are unable to discover or conjecture what effects it might produce. Even after we observe one instance of a particular event followed by another, we are unable to predict what will happen in similar cases. Yet when we find that one particular kind of event is always conjoined with an event of another kind, we no longer hesitate to *expect* that when an event of the first kind occurs, an event of the other kind will occur. We confidently call one object the *cause* and the other the *effect*. In these circumstances, we suppose that the two objects are *connected*. We are certain that there is some *power* in the cause that "infallibly produces" the effect with the "strongest necessity" (EHU 7.2.27). Hume concludes that our idea of necessary connection somehow arises from experiencing the constant conjunction of two kinds of events in a way that observing one instance of cause and effect could never produce.

As we have also noticed before, that there is nothing new in a number of exactly similar instances that is not also there in a single instance. Yet experience of the repetition of similar cases produces something that experience of a single case cannot produce. After many experiences of finding one kind of event constantly conjoined with events of another kind, we associate the two kinds of event, so that when an event of one kind appears, custom or habit leads us to expect an event of the other kind. Hume claims that we are aware of this customary transition of the mind. We have the *feeling* of being determined—caused—to form the belief that the associated event will occur. Our awareness of being determined is the sentiment or internal impression from which we derive our idea of power or necessary connection. When we say that one object is necessarily connected with another, what we mean is that they have acquired a connection in our thoughts. The determination of our minds involved in the inference from our awareness of the cause to our expectation of the effect is the source of our idea of necessary connection. This is what he had in mind when he said in the *Treatise* that "perhaps 'twill appear in the end, that the necessary connexion depends on the inference, instead of the inference's depending on the necessary connexion" (T 1.3.6.3).

Hume has finally discovered the source of our idea of necessary connection. The idea of necessary connection is not only an essential part of our idea of causation, but "that relation is of much greater importance" than the other components of that idea (T 1.3.2.10). He is now ready to sum up his findings, as his account of definition dictates, by giving us "an exact definition" of cause.

He actually gives us *two* definitions. His first definition is:

An object, followed by another, and where all the objects similar to the first are followed by objects similar to the second.

This definition summarizes all the relevant *external impressions* we experience. We pick out an object as the cause of another when similar objects of that kind have been constantly conjoined in our experience with similar objects of another kind. But as we have seen, our external impressions do not exhaust the impressions that make up our idea of causation. We also need to include our *internal impression* of the feeling we have when we are aware of the movement, transition, or determination of our minds from our impression of the cause in the circumstances described in the first definition, to the idea of the associated object. Hume's second definition captures this internal impression. According to it, a cause is

An object followed by another, and whose appearance always conveys the thought to that other.

Since a definition of an idea for Hume is a list of the impressions that compose an idea, both definitions are definitions in Hume's sense. However, his "exact" or "just definition" of our idea of causation is the combination of his two definitions (EHU 7.2.29). Only taken together do they capture *all* of the relevant impressions involved.

We can now see that Hume's account of our idea of causation is more radical than we were able to appreciate fully in our discussion of causal inference. Hume locates the source of the idea of necessary connection *in us*, not in the objects themselves or even in our ideas of those objects we regard as causes and effects. In doing so, Hume completely changes the course of the causation debate, reversing what everyone else thought about the idea of necessary connection. His account was controversial in his day, and it remains so in ours. Every subsequent discussion of causation must begin by confronting the challenges Hume poses for traditional, more metaphysical, ways of looking at our idea of causation.

Hume's treatment of our idea of causation is his flagship illustration of how his method works and the revolutionary results it can achieve. In his subsequent work, he goes on to apply not only his method, but also his concrete results, to other debates and problems that were prominent in the modern period: probable inference, testimony for miracles, the question of intelligent design, and—as we shall see in the next chapter—the debate about liberty and necessity.

7

Liberty and necessity

Hume's treatment of our idea of causation provides an excellent illustration of his account of definition at work as well as an impressive solution to the early modern causation debate. In this chapter, we will see him apply both his method and his solution to the causation debate to another debate, the "long disputed question concerning liberty and necessity" (EHU 8.1.2).

Hume thinks that previous players in the debate regarded it as a clash between rival metaphysical positions, which led them into "a labyrinth of obscure sophistry." However, he regards the question about liberty and necessity as, at bottom, a verbal dispute. He thinks it is high time "to pass from words to the true and real subject of the controversy"—the *ideas* involved (EHU 8.1.1). Hume transforms the debate by refusing to engage with what he takes to be unintelligible metaphysical arguments. The way he will resolve—or better, *dissolve*—the dispute is by using his account of definition to get clear about the content of our *ideas* of liberty and necessity. The key to his dissolution of the dispute is his "new definition of necessity," which "puts the whole controversy in a new light." Since he regards his account of our idea of necessary connection as the only intelligible definition of that idea, he believes that even "the most zealous advocates for free-will must allow this union and inference with regard to human actions" (Abstract 34).

Hume discusses our ideas of liberty and necessity in *Treatise* 2.3.1–2, in Section 8 of the first *Enquiry*, and in the *Abstract*. His accounts are closely parallel; some passages in his *Enquiry* account are taken verbatim from the *Treatise*. The most dramatic difference is in their staging. His *Treatise* discussion is buried in the final part of his account of the passions, some 227 pages after his treatment of necessary connection. In the *Enquiry*, he places his discussion immediately after his account of necessary connection, where he "laid the foundation of his doctrine in what he said concerning cause and effect" (Abstract 31).

Philosophical context: the free will debate

The early modern debate about liberty and necessity concerns the metaphysical status of the freedom or liberty of human actions in a mechanistic universe. Participants in the debate regard its outcome as having significant implications for morality and religion.

Two positions dominate the debate. Both sides accept a mechanistic picture of the universe, and both agree that human actions are free. They differ about the correct way to characterize liberty. Their differences are typically put in terms of a distinction between two kinds of liberty that they inherit from the scholastics. One kind of freedom, *liberty of spontaneity,* is acting as you choose free of any external constraints. In this sense, you may be free even though your choices are completely determined—caused—by your motives, desires, and beliefs. Alice is free in this sense if she chooses the left fork in the road rather than the right because she really wants to see the cherry blossoms, and no one is forcing her to choose the left fork. The other kind of freedom, *liberty of indifference*, is having the ability to determine oneself to choose between alternative courses of action in a particular instance. Alice is free in this sense if she is able to choose whether to turn right or left at the fork, independently of any other determining factors, external or internal, except her own choice.

The most prominent defenders of liberty of spontaneity are Thomas Hobbes and John Locke, both of whom are *compatibilists.* They maintain that human freedom is compatible with the truth of determinism. Although a number of minor theologians oppose compatibilism, the main champion of liberty of indifference is Samuel Clarke. He advocates a form of *libertarianism* according to which voluntary human actions are *self-determined.*

Hobbes is a metaphysical materialist, who thinks that everything in the universe, including the mental capacities and actions of humans, is matter in motion obeying mechanical laws. He claims that the Causal Maxim—the principle that nothing begins without a cause—is self-evident and necessary. Causes necessitate their effects, and a cause not followed by its effect is inconceivable. The necessity involved is logical necessity.

Hobbes calls his brand of metaphysical determinism *the doctrine of necessity*. Everything that happens in the world, including human actions, is brought about by antecedent causes. Even voluntary actions are determined or necessitated. But Hobbes also believes that liberty and necessity are consistent. He opts for a version of liberty of spontaneity, defining freedom as the absence of external impediments—meaning any causal factor that is external to the nature or intrinsic qualities of the agent. For Hobbes, the act of willing is the necessary cause of voluntary actions. A free agent is someone who is not prevented from doing what he has the will to do—nothing external forces him to do what he wills to do. Freedom from constraint is thus compatible with the necessity of action, so morality is not threatened.

Locke's contribution to the debate is a more nuanced version of compatibilism, but the central features of his position closely parallel Hobbes'. Although Locke never flaunts the doctrine of necessity as Hobbes did, as a mechanist who accepts the Causal Maxim, he is committed to it. In Locke's account, a power is defined in terms of the effects it produces, so the necessary connection between a cause and its effect is also a logical connection. As we saw in the last chapter, our *active power*—the ability to make any change—is derived from reflection on the ability of our wills to move our bodies and to consider and dismiss thoughts. Voluntary actions are actions that are directed by an act of willing.

The idea of liberty arises by asking how far the power of our will extends. Locke defines liberty as the power an agent has to do or refrain from doing any particular action "according to the determination of the thought of the mind, when either of them is preferred to the other" (Essay 2.21.8). This definition is close to Hobbes' account of liberty, and commits Locke to the liberty of spontaneity as well, so for him liberty means the absence of external constraint. Although his fully developed position on liberty and necessity is much more subtle than Hobbes', its subtlety was largely lost on the eighteenth-century participants in the debate.

Samuel Clarke argues against the compatibilists that liberty should be characterized as liberty of indifference, since genuine freedom requires a strong libertarian power of *self-determination*, and not just the absence of external constraints. Clarke spends more time criticizing the arguments of his opponents than providing positive arguments for his view. According to him, since God is omnipotent, he has the power to give us the power to determine ourselves. To see that he has done so, he says that we need to reflect *first* on the fact that he has given us intelligence, which gives us the ability to determine which actions are right. The *second* necessary condition for self-determination is self-motion—our power to initiate motion ourselves. We can also see that we have this power because when we act, he claims, what we experience is what we would experience if we had the power of self-motion. Clarke thinks this is enough to show that our wills are free. The power of self-motion together with intelligence is liberty.

The power to choose is provided by the will. In order to will, one must have a judgment about what to do and the power to act in accordance with that judgment. Clarke sometimes calls the will the cause of choosing because its power provides the active component of choice. At other times, he identifies the power of the will with our ability to produce action.

Clarke believes he has shown that we have a self-determining will that can freely assent or refrain from assenting to the mind's judgments. He regards this as a freedom of choosing, not a freedom of acting. For Clarke, a person can be free in the sense of choosing even in prison.

Clarke maintains that if Hobbes' form of determinism were correct, it would destroy our power of self-determination. It may be surprising, then, that he subscribes to the Causal Maxim, but he argues that it is a mistake to hold that liberty is impossible because every event must have a cause. Those who believe that liberty and the Causal Maxim are incompatible fail to distinguish between physical efficient causes—ordinary causes in the material world—and moral motives.

Avoid this confusion and you can see that choices made from moral motives are free, while being morally necessary. Moral necessity, he maintains, is consistent with perfect liberty. We are able to act from reasons that arise solely from our knowledge of moral truths. Our knowledge of the eternal fitnesses and unfitnesses of things provides us with moral motives. Acting morally consists in our ability to be moved by our knowledge of these eternal truths. This ability is at the core of what Clarke calls the freedom of choosing, or sometimes, the power of agency. He believes that the highest form of freedom is to will as one should—having your will in sync with the right values. Self-determination is a necessary condition for this higher form of freedom as well as for religion, since whether your motives are in sync with the right values will determine your fate in the afterlife.

Hume: actions are both necessary and free

Hume explains what he means when he says that "the whole controversy has hitherto turned merely upon words." When metaphysicians argue about liberty and necessity, they use these familiar terms, but they do not stop to consider what their content really is. Since we are all using the same terms, he says that we first need to get clear about what they mean. Doing so will in effect dissolve the controversy. He is confident that when we get clear about the content of our idea of necessity and our idea of liberty, he will be able to show that all of us "have ever agreed in the doctrine both of liberty and necessity" (EHU 8.1.3). A surprising conclusion to a longstanding debate!

Hume begins by examining our idea of necessity. As we have seen, all of the participants in the debate are mechanists, so they agree that necessity applies to the interactions of physical objects. He reminds us what their view amounts to:

> It is universally allowed that matter, in all its operations, is actuated by a necessary force, and that every natural effect is so precisely determined by the energy of its cause that no other effect, in such particular circumstances, could possibly have resulted from it. (EHU 8.1.4; T 2.3.1.3)

What we have to do now, Hume continues, is to get clear about what our idea of *necessity* is when we apply it to physical objects. The way to do that is to consider how we get the idea of physical necessity. Since he spent the previous section of the *Enquiry* doing just that, he reminds us of what he concluded there. The source of our idea of causation and necessity is the uniformity we observe in nature, where we experience objects of one kind constantly conjoined with objects of another kind. When we experience this constant conjunction, our minds are determined by custom to infer that an object of one kind will occur when an object of the other kind appears. He concludes, as he did in the previous section:

> These two circumstances form the whole of that necessity, which we ascribe to matter. Beyond the constant *conjunction* of similar objects, and the consequent *inference* from one to the other, we have no notion of any necessity or connexion. (EHU 8.1.5)

Now that we are clear about our idea of necessity as it applies to physical objects, Hume looks at human actions to see if they are necessitated. He first needs to determine whether we find constant conjunctions between our motives and voluntary actions. If we agree that our motives and actions are constantly conjoined, then the next stage is to determine whether those constant conjunctions are the basis of the inferences we make when we infer someone's motives from their voluntary actions. If it turns out that everyone agrees that these two circumstances are present in our voluntary actions, he can conclude that everyone has always agreed about the doctrine of necessity.

Hume believes that we agree about the constant conjunction part. We are all very much alike. The same motives produce the same actions, and our passions are very similar, no matter what "nation or age" we are from. Human nature has been pretty much the same at all times and places. History is useful because it helps us discover the constant and universal principles of human nature. Studying Roman history teaches us that jealousy, envy, and the desire for power are just as strong motives for the actions of Brutus and Caesar as they are for political leaders today. Historians' records of our past amount to "so many collections of experiments" that provide data for moral philosophers in the same way the experiments of natural philosophers give scientists information about the various plants, animals, and minerals they study (EHU 8.1.7).

That we acknowledge as much uniformity in human motives and actions as we find in the movements of physical objects is shown by the fact that we do not believe travelers' tales that are fantastic or outrageous, or histories that have humans behaving in a manner that is entirely unlike the way we act. When someone tells us that she visited a land where people fly, run faster than locomotives, and leap tall buildings at a single bound, we think she is a liar. If our motives and actions were not so uniform, experience would be useless in regulating our conduct and conducting our affairs.

None of this, of course, means that everybody always acts in *exactly* the same way. We readily grant that the French have a certain *joie de vivre* that the British lack, that citizens of a country governed by a despot behave differently from those who live in a democracy, and that old men have different interests and concerns than young women. We need to allow for the fact that people's characters, prejudices, and beliefs may differ considerably, as do the social, economic, and political circumstances in which they act. Experiencing diversity, however, helps to make our general conclusions about human behavior more fine-grained. If we did not find some uniformity and regularity amid all this diversity, we would not be able to understand anyone's actions, or figure out how we should behave towards others. Besides, the diversity we find in nature and the physical world is just as great as the diversity we find in human actions.

Hume anticipates the objection that there are human actions that we consider irregular and extraordinary. He responds that this is true in the physical world as well. Not all causes are joined to their effects with perfect uniformity. We believe smoking causes lung cancer, even though we are aware that not everyone who smokes gets cancer. Although ordinary people think that the uncertainty in an event reflects an uncertainty in its cause, scientists know that it will be due to the operation of causes that may not be immediately obvious. When a clock suddenly stops, there may not be any obvious cause. But a clockmaker knows to look carefully at the mechanism to determine what has gone wrong.

Physicians have learned that human bodies are complicated, so they look for hidden causes when we behave irregularly. If your usually patient friend replies irascibly to your innocuous question, you conclude that she did not sleep well, or is anxious about a deadline. Someone else, who knows her better, points out that she had her wisdom teeth pulled yesterday, which explains her uncharacteristic response. Even when someone's character seems inconstant and irregular, we suppose that there is some underlying cause that operates in a uniform manner, just as we suppose that the seemingly capricious changes in the weather are governed by regular principles we have not as yet discovered.

Hume says that his examination establishes that the conjunctions between our motives and actions are as regular and uniform as the conjunctions we find in the natural world. He adds that the ease with which he has produced this evidence shows that we have always been aware of the regularity.

Having established that there are regular conjunctions between our motives and actions, Hume's next step is to show that this *uniformity* between motives and actions is the source of the *inferences* we make concerning human actions. He points out that we make inferences about the actions of others so routinely in our everyday thinking that we are not really aware that this is what we are doing. Philosophers do the same thing. These inferences are also essential to other branches of the arts and sciences. Drama critics evaluate the author of a play according to whether the conduct and sentiments of his characters are natural or unnatural. Political science depends on the supposition that laws and forms of government have a uniform influence upon society. We determine the accuracy of a historian on the basis of how what he says fits with our experience of humankind. Hume concludes that it seems impossible "to engage either in science or action of any kind without acknowledging the doctrine of necessity, and this *inference* from motives to voluntary actions, from character to conduct" (EHU 8.1.18).

When we explain actions, we often link *natural* or physical evidence and *moral* evidence—evidence concerning human actions, beliefs, and motives—together in chains of reasoning. When we do, we do not distinguish the two sorts of evidence as differing in kind or certainty when we go from one link in the chain to another. The conjunctions to which the two sorts of evidence appeal have the same effects on our minds. Explaining why a prisoner is unable to escape might equally refer to his inability to chisel through the walls of his cell and his lack of success in bribing the jailer.

Hume imagines an objector trying to break the parallel between natural and moral evidence by arguing that human action is far more capricious than he has portrayed it. Surely, he asks, for all you know, your closest friend might suddenly go ballistic and threaten to kill you for not serving him his favorite dessert. Hume responds by granting that, since this is a point about a matter of fact, it is indeed *possible*. But in the same sense of *possible*, it is also possible that a sudden earthquake might level my house. My certainty that my friend will not put his hand in the fire and hold it there until it is completely burned up is no different from my certainty that if he jumps out my window, he will fall to the ground instead of floating up and away like a feather. Both are questions of fact, and both are possible, but the possibility does not reduce my certainty that neither will happen. The parallel between natural and moral evidence remains.

At this point, Hume is satisfied that he has shown that the sense of necessity we attribute to the interactions of physical objects also applies to the relations between human actions and motives. Both are based on observed regular conjunctions, which produce our inferences from object to object, and from action to motive. He has also shown that our ordinary, as well as our more philosophical, ascriptions of the relations between actions and motives follow this pattern. Everyone's behavior "without hesitation" thus shows that they acknowledge, at least tacitly, that the sense of necessity is the same in both physical and moral cases (EHU 8.1.21).

This raises a puzzle. "What could possibly be the reason," Hume asks, why we have "such a reluctance to acknowledge [the doctrine of necessity] in words, and have rather shown a propensity, in all ages, to profess the contrary opinion" (EHU 8.1.21). His diagnosis is that in cases of physical causation, we find that we can never go farther than observing that when we have experienced the constant conjunction of particular kinds of objects, our minds are carried by a customary transition from the appearance of one object to belief in the other. But notwithstanding that this conclusion is

> the result of the strictest scrutiny of this subject, men still entertain a strong propensity to believe that they penetrate farther into the powers of nature, and perceive something like a necessary connection between the cause and the effect. (EHU 8.1.21)

Hume attributes this desire to the temptation to do metaphysics—to discover the "ultimate principles" that lie behind experience. He rests his case on the reminder that he has already shown that the claims of the leading contenders to provide such a necessary connection are unintelligible. Those who think they can make sense of a stronger connection between cause and effect need to deliver the goods. He is confident that they will fail. He has given us the only intelligible sense of that idea by tracing it to its two sources in impressions.

With that, Hume turns to our idea of *liberty*. He thinks he can show that everyone has always agreed about that idea as well, which will be further confirmation that the dispute has been "merely verbal." When we apply the term *liberty* to our voluntary actions, he argues that we cannot mean that our actions have so little connection with our motives, inclinations, and circumstances that one does not follow regularly from the other, and that the one does not lead us to infer the other, since the regular connection and our inferences are "plain and acknowledged matters of fact." Given these facts, Hume thinks that by liberty we must mean what we saw Hobbes and Locke defending as the *liberty of spontaneity*, namely: "*a power of acting or not acting, according to the determinations of the will*." You have liberty of spontaneity—*freedom*—in this sense when there is nothing external to you forcing you to do something, or when there are no external forces that prevent you from doing what you choose to do. Many of our actions are free in this sense. Most mornings you get out of bed when you decide to, not because someone drags you out of it. You eat a bowl of ice cream when you choose to, if no one is preventing you from eating it or has eaten the last available ice cream. As Hume says, this kind of liberty "is universally allowed to belong to everyone who is not a prisoner and in chains" (EHU 8.1.23). It is the most common sense of liberty as well as the only coherent sense of the term. In this sense, liberty or freedom is not opposed to the view that human actions are determined—caused.

Hume's diagnosis of the debate

Hume concludes his discussion by offering a diagnosis of why ordinary people have mistakenly assumed that believing that an action is necessary is incompatible with believing that it is free. He thinks that there are two general reasons behind this assumption. The first is that some claim that while some causes are necessary, others are not necessary. Hume is alluding to *the doctrine of liberty*, which we saw was traditionally called *liberty of indifference*, and was primarily championed in Britain by Samuel Clarke. According to this view, liberty is *self-determination*, or the freedom to determine your own will. Hume argues that the doctrine of liberty is based on a misunderstanding of our idea of liberty, and is actually incoherent. Liberty, in this sense, "means a negation of necessity and causes." Self-determination is supposed to be a non-necessitating cause that determines your will. For Hume, a "cause" without necessity is no cause at all. In rejecting necessity, the libertarian is rejecting causation as well. What is left is not determination, then, but chance, "which is universally allowed to have no existence" (EHU 8.1.25). Denying that our actions are caused is equivalent to saying that they happen by chance.

The second reason why people have denied the doctrine of necessity stems from religion, which has been "very unnecessarily interested in this question" (T 2.3.2.3). One tactic frequently employed in philosophical debates during the modern period was to try to disprove a claim by arguing that it has dangerous consequences for religion or morality. Libertarians argue that the doctrine of necessity is a threat to religion and morality and dismiss it for this reason. According to them, if our actions are necessitated, we are no longer responsible for them and, consequently, we should not be morally praised and blamed. But as Hume reminds us, a view is not false just because it poses a threat.

Hume's response is to turn the tables on the champions of the doctrine of liberty. He argues that it is the libertarian conception of necessity and liberty that poses a threat to religion and morality, not his conception. In fact, our ideas of both necessity and liberty, if correctly defined, are essential to them.

Hume has two arguments to show why *necessity* is essential to religion and morality. The first is that it is required, if the practice of punishing and rewarding people is to make sense. One way to motivate people to obey laws is with sanctions. Sanctions are rewards (pleasures) or punishments (pains) that human beings or God use to motivate us to act in certain ways. They include such things as remaining free or going to jail, going to heaven or being sent to hell. Punishing and rewarding, however, would not work to motivate people to obey laws, unless actions were caused. Sanctions influence people's actions in predictable ways, which is why it makes sense to use them. For example, the threat of jail deters people from breaking the law, but if this threat was administered randomly, it would not work as a deterrent. If human actions were not caused, sanctions would no longer work in predictable ways and the practice would no longer make sense.

The second, and more important, reason why necessity is required is that we cannot make sense of the idea that it is morally *fair* to blame and punish people, unless we are able to hold them responsible for their actions. The doctrine of necessity, Hume argues, is required if we are to hold people responsible for what they do.

> Actions are, by their very nature, temporary and perishing; and where they proceed not from some *cause* in the character and disposition of the person who performed them, they can neither redound to his honour, if good; nor infamy, if evil. The actions themselves may be blameable; they may be contrary to all the rules of morality and religion: But the person is not answerable for them ... as they proceeded from nothing in him that is durable or constant. (EHU 8.2.29; T 2.3.2.6)

We properly blame someone for an evil action only if we regard her as responsible for her actions. We hold someone responsible only if we regard the person herself as the cause of her actions. And to do that, we need to see the person's actions as springing from durable and constant features of her character.

According to Hume, libertarians claim that human actions are free in the sense that they are uncaused. He takes that to mean that actions do not proceed from anything in a person's character. But if the connection between the person and the action is broken, libertarians can no longer make sense of the idea that an agent's action is *her* action:

> according to the doctrine of liberty or chance, this connexion is reduc'd to nothing, nor are men more accountable for those actions, which are design'd and premeditated, than for such as are the most casual and accidental. (T 2.3.2.6)

If an agent's actions are not imputable to her, it is no longer fair to blame and punish her for her bad actions. But on the libertarian view, Hume reminds us, a man is as pure and untainted, after having committed the most horrid crimes, as at the first moment of his birth, nor is his character any way concern'd in his actions; since they are not derived from it, and the wickedness of one can never be us'd as a proof of the depravity of the other. (T 2.3.2.6; EHU 8.2.29)

If a person's actions do not spring from her character, they can no longer serve as "proof" of her morally bad character, so it is no longer fair to judge her to be a bad person on the basis of her bad actions.

Similarly, actions must be necessitated, if we are to make sense of such things as repenting (T 2.3.2.7). An agent repents when she recognizes that she acted badly, feels sorry about it, and attempts to mend her ways. But unless the agent sees her past "criminal" acts as actions for which she is responsible, it does not make sense for her to feel sorry that she did them. To repent, she needs to see them as hers, as proceeding from her criminal character. Why repent when my behavior is not connected to me or happens by chance? We can only make sense of the fact that "repentance wipes off every crime," if we acknowledge that

actions render a person criminal merely as they are proofs of criminal principles in the mind; and when, by an alteration of these principles, they cease to be just proofs, they likewise cease to be criminal. (EHU 8.2.30; T 2.3.2. 7)

The problem with the libertarian position is that the criminal actions "never were just proofs, and consequently never were criminal." They cannot make sense of such ordinary acts as repenting.

Hume thinks it is easy to show that *liberty of spontaneity* is essential to morality. If we find out that a person was forced or compelled to do something by something external to him, we no longer hold him responsible and praise or blame him. He has in mind such ordinary cases as bumping into the person next to you because the bus lurches, or falling on someone because you were blown by the wind. In cases such as these, you are a conduit for forces external to you, and we do not hold someone responsible if she is a mere conduit. We hold a person responsible and praise or blame him only if we regard his actions as springing from durable features of his character and nothing prevented him from doing what he chose to do. This is the only sort of liberty, he claims, that matters to us.

Hume is satisfied that in concluding his study of "the question of liberty and necessity; the most contentious question of metaphysics, the most contentious science," he has shown that the dispute is actually a verbal one—not a question of metaphysics at all (EHU 8.1.23). Once we get clear about the content of our ideas of necessity and liberty, it is clear that everyone actually agrees that human actions are both necessary and free. Despite Hume's youthful confidence that he has dissolved this longstanding debate, philosophers continue to argue about whether human actions are necessary or free or are both necessary and free. Hume scholars disagree about how to interpret Hume's dissolution of the debate. They also disagree about whether this is a metaphysical debate or a debate about our ideas of liberty and necessity.

8

Against moral rationalism

Hume steps into an ongoing debate about ethics, often called the British Moralists debate, which began in the mid-seventeenth century and continued until the end of the eighteenth. Three types of theories are represented in this debate: self-interest theories, rationalist theories, and sentimentalist theories. Hume became the most famous proponent of sentimentalism. The different players in the debate helped shape his understanding both of the problems to be addressed and their possible solutions. He uses the same method here as he does in the debate about causation: there is a *critical phase* in which he argues against his opponents and a *constructive phase* in which he presents his version of sentimentalism.

In this chapter, we outline the British Moralists debate, briefly describing the views of representatives of these three types of moral theories, and then turn to Hume's arguments in his *critical phase* against moral rationalism. In Chapters 9 and 10, we discuss his concerns in the *constructive phase*—the version of sentimentalism Hume develops and defends as well as his explanations of the natural virtues and the artificial virtue of justice.

Philosophical context: the British moralists debate

Thomas Hobbes' (1588–1679) brilliant but shocking attempt to derive moral and political obligation from motives of self-interest initiated a sustained philosophical debate. His *Leviathan*, first published in 1651, was as controversial then as it is now. Hobbes, as his contemporaries and successors understood him, characterizes us as naturally self-centered creatures, concerned to preserve ourselves and increase our power. Power is the means to self-preservation, but since power is secured only by more power, the search for it is bottomless. In the state of nature, a pre-moral and pre-legal state, we seek to preserve ourselves by trying to dominate others. Since we are equally powerful, this results in a war of all against all in which life is "solitary, poor, nasty, brutish, and short" (L 13.9; BM vol 1 37). The way out is to make a contract with one another. We agree to hand over our power to a sovereign, who makes the laws that are necessary for us to live together peaceably and who also has the power to make us comply with them. These laws, along with the enforcement mechanism, ensure peace, which is in each person's interest. The political state and moral obligation come into being only with an empowered sovereign. In the state of nature, there is no right or wrong, justice or injustice.

This reading of Hobbes was reinforced by the appearance of Bernard Mandeville's (1670–1733) *The Fable of the Bees* in 1714. In one of its essays, "An Enquiry into the Origin of Moral Virtue," he provides a natural history of morality. He claims that human beings in their natural state are selfish, headstrong, and unruly. Some clever politicians, however, recognizing that we need to live in a civilized society, took up the task of domesticating us. They set out to dupe us into believing that we should conquer our selfish passions and help others. Realizing that we are proud creatures, highly susceptible to praise and blame, they were able to motivate many of us to live up to the ideal of virtue by dispensing praise and blame. Mandeville insists that it was not religion but the "skilful Management of wary Politicians" that originally made us tractable. He concludes that the "Moral Virtues are the Political Offspring which Flattery begot upon Pride" (Enquiry 14). Moral concepts are just a tool politicians use to tame us.

Hobbes, especially when understood through the lens of Mandeville, managed to offend almost everyone. Protests against him came not only from academics, but also from members of the British court and Parliament as well as the clergy. People were repelled by his depiction of us as self-centered creatures. They thought his claim that there is no right and wrong in the state of nature was a challenge to the reality of morality. To be called a Hobbist was equivalent to being called an atheist, a materialist, and an immoral brute. The outcry against Mandeville was even shriller. As a more cynical reincarnation of Hobbes, he was thought to be an advocate for immorality and irreligion.

Two kinds of moral theory developed in reaction to Hobbes and Mandeville—rationalism and sentimentalism. While both rationalists and empiricists vehemently opposed the self-interest theories, especially Hobbes', they objected to different parts of these theories.

The rationalists: Clarke and Wollaston

One philosopher especially offended by Hobbes' account of morality was Samuel Clarke (1675–1729). In the second volume of his *Discourse on Natural Religion* (1706) he defends a type of moral rationalism against what he took to be Hobbes' skeptical attack on morality. Hobbes claimed that there is no right or wrong in the state of nature. Clarke took him to be saying that right and wrong are the result of a human convention—a contract—and thus that they are a mere invention and are unreal. The problem with Hobbes' explanation, as Clarke sees it, is that it is a threat to our commitment to morality. If it is the contract that obligates us, what obligates us to keep the contract?

Clarke sets out "to prove and establish the eternal difference of good and evil," a task he would not have had to take up

> had there not appeared certain men, as Mr. Hobbes ... who have presumed ... to assert ... that there is no such difference originally, necessarily, and absolutely in the nature of things. (BM vol 1 194)

The only way to defend morality against skeptical attacks is to ground good and evil in the "nature of things."

Clarke believes there are demonstrable moral relations that are knowable a priori by reason alone. The idea that there are demonstrable moral relations rests on the assumption that each kind of thing has an essential nature that is also knowable by reason alone. The essential natures of things determine the different eternal and necessary relations in which we stand to others and to God. These relations, in turn, make actions fit or unfit, appropriate or inappropriate:

> there is a fitness or suitableness of certain circumstances to certain persons, and an unsuitableness of others; founded in the nature of things and the qualifications of persons ... (BM vol 1 192)

Fitness, as Clarke conceives it, is a relation that holds between actions, persons, and their situations.

We can get a somewhat better idea of what Clarke means by fitness, if we look at some of his examples. He says that since God is infinitely superior to us, it is "certainly fit" that we should worship and obey him (BM vol 1 193). Likewise, since human beings are equal, it is fitting that they should treat each other fairly, just as God's superiority makes it fitting that we should obey him.

Clarke frequently draws an analogy between morality and mathematics to show that moral truths are as self-evident, certain, and knowable as mathematical truths. Consider the axiom that a whole is greater than one of its parts. As long as you know what the terms in it mean, you know that the axiom is true and certain. We do not need to engage in any sort of research or observe anything to see that it is true. Its truth is immediately evident to reason by itself. The fitness and unfitness of actions is self-evident, certain, and knowable in the same way. By looking at the different relations different people stand to one another in different situations, we are able to tell immediately that certain actions are fit and others are unfit. Denying the fitness of certain actions is like denying the axiom that the whole is greater than one of its parts.

Clarke also objects to Hobbes' idea—or what he thinks is Hobbes' idea—that the good person is motivated to obey moral laws by the threat of punishment. Genuinely virtuous action is rational action, and we do not need to be prodded by sanctions to do what we already have a reason to do. The rational intuition that an action is fitting is by itself a motive to perform the action. On Clarke's view, the morally good person is motivated to do what is right by the motive of duty—because it is self-evident to reason that the action is fitting.

Clarke appeals to reason to explain almost every facet of morality. Moral principles are self-evident principles of reason. To act morally is the same as acting rationally. The rational awareness that an action is fit has the power both to obligate us and to motivate us.

At one point, Clarke says that evildoers, by opposing the nature and relations of things, "endeavor ... to make things be what they are not, and cannot be," which he thinks is as absurd as trying to change a mathematical truth (BM vol 1 201). William Wollaston (1660–1724) constructs his entire moral theory around this idea. Unlike Clarke, for whom the basic moral notions are fitness and unfitness, Wollaston argues that moral goodness and evil may be reduced to truth and falsehood. His only philosophical work, *Religion of Nature Delineated* (1724), was extremely popular during his life, but his theory was often misinterpreted. His most remembered and also most misunderstood claim is that an evildoer "*lives a lie*" (BM vol 1 242).

Wollaston's primary aim was to find a rule that will allow us to distinguish right actions from wrong actions. He has a two-part argument. In the first part, he begins by defining true propositions as those that "express things as they are" (BM vol 1 240). He then argues that we are able to say things not only with words, but also with our actions. Since we may assert or deny propositions with our actions, actions may be true or false. He means more by this than that we are able to understand gestures such as laughing, weeping, or shrugging. To use his example, if one group of soldiers fires on another, the first group's actions assert that the second group is its enemy. If the second group is not the first group's enemy, its assertion is false.

In the second part of his argument, Wollaston proposes what he thinks is the basic criterion of immoral actions: "*No act ... that interferes with any true proposition, or denies any thing to be as it is, can be right*" (BM vol 1 243). Immoral actions deny things to be what they are, and, thus, express false propositions. If I break a promise, I falsely declare that I never made one. If I drive off in your car, I falsely declare that it is mine. To treat things as being what they are not, Wollaston says, is as irrational and absurd as denying that 2 + 2 = 4.

Wollaston claims that since we are rational creatures, reason ought to govern us. Reason by itself should move us to perform right actions, or, at least, to refrain from performing immoral actions. Like Clarke, Wollaston believes that reason by itself enables us to know which actions are right and that it has the power to motivate us to do them.

Although Hume argues against Wollaston's view, Clarke is his main opponent. Clarke is the first in a long line to defend what today is called *moral realism*. According to that view, moral entities, facts or properties are mind-independent in the sense that they are conceived as existing over and above our perceptions. On a realist picture, actions would be right or wrong, fit or unfit, even if no one could have any conception that they were so. The rightness and wrongness, fitness and unfitness are there for reason to discover. Clarke thinks of moral relations as being "out there"—as part of the framework of the universe. Philosophers continue to this day to defend the kind of realism that Clarke endorsed in response to what they regard as skeptical attacks on morality.

The sentimentalists: Shaftesbury and Hutcheson

The other type of theory that developed in reaction to Hobbes and Mandeville is sentimentalism. Besides Hume, the other sentimentalists include Anthony Ashley Cooper, Third Earl of Shaftesbury (1671–1713), and Francis Hutcheson (1694–1746). Joseph Butler (1692–1752) is also sometimes considered a sentimentalist since there are features of sentimentalism in his moral theory. All three philosophers wrote before Hume and influenced his sentimentalism. Adam Smith (1723–90), the famous economist, was Hume's sentimentalist successor.

The sentimentalists were as offended by Hobbes and Mandeville as the rationalists, but they criticize different parts of the self-interest theories. They oppose Hobbes' and Mandeville's characterization of us as naturally selfish and self-absorbed creatures, arguing that we genuinely care about others for their own sakes. Other-regarding affections such as benevolence, compassion, love, and gratitude are original and real parts of human nature. They emphasize the fact that we are by nature social creatures. They also object to the idea that moral judgments are based in self-interest, arguing that moral approval and disapproval spring from a disinterested source.

According to sentimentalism, the locus of value—what has value—are certain first-order sentiments, the passions and affections that directly motivate people to act and the actions that express them. The source of value—what makes them morally good or bad—are our reflective, second-order sentiments about our own or other people's sentiments. The second-order sentiments are distinctive feelings of approbation and disapprobation. Hutcheson construes approval and disapproval as a special kind of love and hatred. To feel approbation or love is to esteem others—having a high regard for them. Approval and disapproval give rise to the basic ideas of moral goodness and badness. When we approve of the motive of generosity, we judge it to be morally good as well as the actions to which it gives rise. We also judge the character trait—being a generous person—from which the motive springs as morally good or virtuous.

At one point, Shaftesbury calls our second-order reflective capacity to have sentiments about sentiments a *moral sense*. Hutcheson picks up the idea of a moral sense and makes it central to his theory. Just as we are able to see things because we have the sense of sight and hear things because we have the sense of hearing, so too we are able to immediately and directly "perceive" motives and actions as being morally good or bad because we possess a moral sense. The moral sense disposes us to feel approval or disapproval immediately when we contemplate people's character traits. Hutcheson thinks the claim that we have a unique moral sense follows from two other claims. One is Locke's claim that every simple idea comes from a sense. The other is that the basic moral ideas of goodness and badness are simple ideas, a claim many philosophers during this period accept.

Hutcheson argues that we approve of only one type of affection—benevolence, the desire to promote the good of others. The four cardinal virtues—temperance, courage, prudence, and justice—are virtues only when they are governed by benevolence. For instance, temperance—not drinking or eating too much—is not morally good unless it makes us better able to serve humankind. Similarly, courage—standing your ground in the face of danger—is not morally good unless it makes us better able to face danger when defending innocent people.

Although Hutcheson believes that there is only one kind of virtue—benevolence—he distinguishes among three types. The morally best sort is Christian love—calm, universal benevolence that aims at the good of everyone. Benevolence when directed towards smaller groups such as family, neighbors, or fellow citizens, as well as particular kind feelings of love, pity, and sympathy, are also good, but to a lesser extent. They are good, but only if they do not counteract universal benevolence.

Both Shaftesbury and Hutcheson believe that human nature is on the whole good. Hutcheson, for example, says that human beings are not really capable of disinterested malice—desiring the misery of others. When we act badly, it is not because we have bad passions, but because our passions are out of balance. We disapprove when someone's concern for himself is so strong that it overpowers his concern for others. We also disapprove when someone's concern for others is so weak that she is no longer moved by the plight of others.

Hutcheson's moral theory is deeply Christian. Morality, for him, is essentially a matter of love. What we approve of most is the calm Christian love that aims at promoting the good of everyone. The feeling of approbation, as he construes it, is a special kind of love.

The sentimentalist theory is often said to represent an "inward" turn since, for the sentimentalists, morality springs from our nature. What has value in the first instance are certain first-order passions and sentiments, but what makes them valuable are our second-order sentiments of approval and disapproval. Morality, for the sentimentalists, is entirely a product of human nature.

Hutcheson was the first sentimentalist to argue in a systematic way not only against self-interest theorists, but also against moral rationalists. In his first major work, *An Inquiry into the Original of our Ideas of Beauty and Virtue* (1725), he opposes the self-interest theories of Hobbes and Mandeville. In a later work, *Illustrations on the Moral Sense* (1728), he objects to the rationalist theories of Clarke and Wollaston, among other rationalists.

Hume reverses this order. In the *Treatise*, he opposes moral rationalism. In the second *Enquiry*, he continues to object to moral rationalism, but he also opposes self-interest theories. Since Hume's main target is moral rationalism, in the next section we examine his arguments against it. In Chapters 9 and 10 we briefly look at some of his arguments against self-interest theories. Hutcheson's influence on Hume in his critical phase was enormous. Hume follows Hutcheson both in the way in which he understands his opponents and the way in which he characterizes the debate between them. Hutcheson was a brilliant arguer and Hume freely borrows many of his arguments against these opponents.

Arguments against moral rationalism

As the eighteenth century progressed, philosophers argued less with Hobbes and Mandeville, and more with each other. By the time Hume wrote the *Treatise*, he assumed that the self-interest theories had been adequately refuted. If they are no longer on the table, there are only two possibilities for him to consider—moral rationalism and sentimentalism. If one falls, the other stands. Hume's strategy dictates that he must first show that moral rationalism fails before he can present his sentimentalist account of morality. His arguments against moral rationalism are found in *Treatise* 3.1.1 and in Appendix 1 of *An Enquiry concerning the Principles of Morals*.

Hume's interpretation of moral rationalism

Hume follows Hutcheson in translating moral rationalism into a sentimentalist framework. One surprising advantage the sentimentalists had over the moral rationalists is that they had a more fully developed view of reason. They reinterpret rationalism in terms of their empiricist conception of reason. Hume tends to characterize reason in two ways. The first is that reason compares ideas to find relations among them. Recall that Hume calls these *philosophical relations*, and there are two types of them—a priori relations of ideas and matters of fact. The second way Hume characterizes reason is that it consists in the discovery of truth or falsehood. He puts Clarke in the group who think that morality is based on some a priori relation of ideas, which seems fair enough, since Clarke claims that the fitness of actions follows from eternal and necessary relations that are intuitively evident to reason. He puts Wollaston in the group who think that reason consists in discovering truth or falsehood.

There is another important way in which Hume follows Hutcheson in translating the rationalists into a sentimentalist framework. Like Hutcheson, he bases morality on the feelings of a *spectator*. Roughly speaking, we may distinguish two different aspects of a moral theory—a *spectator* component and an *agent* component. The spectator component is primarily concerned with answering questions that arise when we assess or evaluate people: how we judge people's characters and motives, when it is appropriate to hold them responsible and to praise or blame them, and who the morally good person is. The agent component is primarily concerned with answering questions that arise when we deliberate: what should or ought I to do? Every complete moral theory should include a discussion of both components, although philosophers tend to privilege one or the other.

Hume privileges the spectator component. He builds his moral theory around the idea of a spectator who approves and disapproves of people's character traits and motives. He thus offers a theory about which character traits and motives are morally good and bad—a theory of virtue and vice. For Hume, as for Hutcheson, the sentiments of approval and disapproval are the source of our ideas of moral goodness and badness. To judge a character trait as morally good or bad is to say it is virtuous or vicious.

Clarke and Wollaston, however, privilege the agent component. They build their theories around the idea of an agent who is trying to decide which actions are right or wrong, fit or unfit. Hume, however, follows Hutcheson in thinking that the rationalists privilege the spectator component. He assumes that they offer rival theories of approval and disapproval and that approval and disapproval apply in the first instance to people's character traits and motives. On Hume's reading of the rationalists, they are concerned to explain how we distinguish virtuous character traits and motives from vicious ones. This interpretation is a distortion of Clarke's and Wollaston's moral theories.

The foundational debate: reason or sentiment?

During this period, moral philosophers assume that there is general agreement about the content of morality. We know more or less what is right or wrong, morally good or bad. They also agree that the basic moral ideas are simple and cannot be defined in terms of their component parts. Even though moral concepts cannot be defined this way, Hume thinks we can explain how we come to have moral concepts.

Recall that Clarke, as a moral realist, thinks that actions would be fit or unfit even if no one could have any intuition that they were so. The fitnesses or unfitnesses of actions exist independently of us and are there for reason to discover. Hume, however, denies that we have access to anything but ideas and impressions, so he thinks that the sort of realism Clarke articulated is not merely false, but incoherent. For him, it is incoherent to think that we can grasp anything that goes beyond the bounds of experience. Since Hume views Clarke's realism as incoherent, he transforms the debate between rationalism and sentimentalism into a debate about the *origin* of our moral concepts. Do our basic moral ideas spring from reason alone or do they spring from sentiment?

Hume frames the debate between rationalism and sentimentalism in terms of his own theory of the mind. If all the contents of the mind are perceptions, to engage in any type of mental activity—seeing, judging, thinking, or loving—is to have some perception before the mind. Similarly, "to approve of one character, to condemn another, are only so many different perceptions" (T 3.1.1. 2). Since there are only two types of perceptions—ideas and impressions—the question between rationalism and sentimentalism is

> *Whether 'tis by means of our* ideas *or* impressions *we distinguish betwixt vice and virtue, and pronounce an action blameable or praise-worthy?* (T 3.1.1.3)

Hume offers a battery of arguments against moral rationalism. His most famous argument, the argument from motivation, relies on an argument he gives earlier in Book II of the *Treatise,* in the section entitled "Of the influencing motives of the will." He argues that the idea of rational action, like the idea of a free or uncaused action, is incoherent. This argument is important in its own right and continues to be influential. We examine this argument before turning to his other arguments against moral rationalism. His case against moral rationalism consists of five main arguments:

1. The argument from the influencing motives of the will (T 2.3.3)
2. The argument from motivation (T 3.1.1. 4–6)
3. The arguments from truth and falsehood (T 3.1.1.9–16)
4. The argument from relations of ideas or matters of fact (T 3.1.1.18–26)
5. The "Is–Ought" argument (T 3.1.1. 27)

It is important to realize that there are different types of moral rationalism and that Hume's arguments are directed at only one type—the sort of realism that Clarke defends. According to him, morality is part of the framework of the universe. While reason tells us what actions are fit or unfit, the relations on which they are based exist prior to and independently of reason. This sort of rationalism should be distinguished from the type Immanuel Kant (1724–1804) went on to develop. On Kant's view, the principles of reason are not part of the fabric of the universe, but are principles that our minds generate, which we then apply to the world around us and to ourselves.

The idea of rational action is nonsense

Nothing is more common, Hume says, than for philosophers and even for people in common life to talk about a combat between reason and passion. They say that we ought to govern our conduct by reason rather than passion. If our passions are not in line with reason's commands, we ought to restrain them or bring them into conformity with reason. They tout the "eternity, invariableness, and divine origin" of reason, while emphasizing the "blindness, unconstancy, and deceitfulness" of our passions. Both ancient and modern philosophy is based on the idea that to act virtuously is to govern your conduct by reason. Hume challenges this view, arguing first that "reason alone can never be a motive to any action of the will" and second, that "it can never oppose passion in the direction of the will" (T 2.3.3.1).

Hume's first and main argument rests on his empiricist conception of reason. Reason consists in finding relations among ideas or in establishing matters of fact. He considers mathematical reasoning from the category of relation of ideas and causal reasoning from the category of matters of fact. He asks us to look at instances of action where these two types of reasoning have an influence and argues that when we do, we will see that reason alone could not have moved us.

No one thinks that mathematical reasoning by itself is capable of moving us. Suppose you want to stay out of debt. You calculate how much money you are owed, how much you owe others, and how much you have saved, to help you stay out of debt. In this case, it is the desire to stay out of debt that provides motivational force. Mathematical reasoning by itself does not move us to do anything. When it has an influence on action, mathematical reasoning is always used in connection with achieving some purpose. It is thus used in connection with causal reasoning, which consists in discovering the means—or causes—to our ends. So Hume asks whether causal reasoning by itself is able to move us to act.

Hume, however, argues that when causal reasoning figures in the production of action, it always presupposes some pre-existing desire or want. On his view, reasoning is a process that moves you from one idea to another idea. If reasoning is to have motivational force, one of the ideas must be tied to some desire or affection. As he says:

> It can never in the least concern us to know, that such objects are causes, and such others effects, if both the causes and effects be indifferent to us. Where the objects themselves do not affect us, their connexion can never give them such influence; and 'tis plain, that as reason is nothing but the discovery of this connexion, it cannot be by its means that the objects are able to affect us. (T 2.3.3.3)

Noticing the causal connection between exercise and losing weight will not move you to exercise unless you want to lose weight. By itself, reason cannot give rise to a motive.

Hume thinks it immediately follows that reason alone cannot oppose a passion in the direction of the will. To oppose a passion, reason must be able to give rise to a motive by itself, since only a motive can oppose another motive. But he has just shown that reason by itself is not able to give rise to a motive. It follows from these two arguments that the idea of a combat between reason and passion is nonsensical. He concludes on an inflammatory note that "Reason is, and ought only to be the slave of the passions, and can never pretend to any other office than to serve and obey them" (T 2.3.3.4).

Hume offers another argument that relies on his characterization of reason as discovering truth and falsehood. Nothing can be unreasonable or contrary to reason, unless it is contrary to truth. Reason judges ideas to be true or false because ideas copy or represent impressions. Passions and emotions, however, are original existences or modifications of existence and do not represent or copy anything. When I am angry, I experience that feeling, but my anger does not represent anything. Since passions do not copy or represent anything, strictly speaking, they cannot be true or false, reasonable or unreasonable.

Hume thinks, however, that passions, in an extended sense, may be reasonable or unreasonable. A passion may be unreasonable if the judgment that accompanies it is false or unreasonable. He distinguishes two types of cases. The first is when a passion is based on a belief that an object exists when in fact it does not, for example, when I reach for what I believe is a glass of wine, but it is really a glass of turpentine. The second is when "we chuse means insufficient for the design'd end, and deceive ourselves in our judgment of causes and effects" (T 2.3.3.6). In this sort of case, the action is based on a false belief either about its cause or effect. For example, I want to lose weight, so I skip breakfast, but that is counterproductive as a means to weight loss, since my metabolism does not get jump-started. In both cases, it is the judgment that accompanies the action that is unreasonable, not the passion. He concludes provocatively that it is not contrary to reason for me "to prefer the destruction of the whole world to the scratching of my finger" (T 2.3.3.6). It is not contrary to reason to choose my own ruin to prevent a stranger from feeling uneasy. Nor is it contrary to reason to prefer an immediate pleasure to my long-term interest.

Hume is aware that he is challenging a well-entrenched and cherished view about the role of reason in action, one almost everyone accepts. He thus needs to explain why virtually everyone is mistaken. One explanation is that we forget that it is the accompanying judgment that is unreasonable, rather than the passion. Another is that our calm passions "produce little emotion in the mind" (T 2.3.3.8). When these calm passions oppose our more violent passions, we mistake this for a conflict between reason and passion, since reason also "exerts itself without producing any sensible emotion" (T 2.3.3.8). Hume does not deny that we experience such everyday conflicts as wanting to eat more ice cream, "knowing" we shouldn't. He only rejects a rationalist understanding of such conflicts.

These arguments have generated considerable debate about the role of reason in action. In his ethical writings, Kant took up the challenge Hume poses and tried to show that reason by itself may move us. Philosophers to this day continue to argue about whether the idea of rational action makes sense. Are there rational norms that apply to our conduct? Some philosophers think that, rationally speaking, we ought to act prudently, acting in ways that promote our own good. If a person acts in ways that are self-destructive, she is acting irrationally. But Hume insists that a person who continues to smoke is not, strictly speaking, acting unreasonably. As he says, it is not contrary to reason to act on my immediate desire for a cigarette, ignoring what is obviously in my best interest, if that is what I prefer.

The argument from motivation

Hume's most well-known argument against moral rationalism, which he thinks is decisive, is the argument from motivation. It is directed primarily against Clarke and has only two premises. The first is that moral ideas have pervasive practical and psychological effects on us, which both experience and philosophy confirm. Experience shows that we are often motivated to perform an action because we think it is obligatory or to refrain from performing an action because we think it is unjust. We try to cultivate the virtues in ourselves and are proud when we succeed and ashamed when we fail. If morality did not have these effects on our passions and actions, moral rules and precepts would be pointless, as would our efforts to cultivate the virtues. Philosophy is commonly divided into two kinds, speculative and practical, and philosophers classify morality as practical because moral ideas have these practical effects. As Hume puts the first premise, "morals excite passions, and produce or prevent actions"(T 3.1.1.6).

The second premise is that by itself reason is incapable of exciting passions or moving us to act or to refrain from acting. This premise is supported by the arguments we just looked at about the influencing motives of the will. The argument from motivation, then, is that if moral concepts are capable of exciting passions and producing or preventing actions, but reason alone is incapable of doing these things, then moral concepts do not spring from reason alone. If moral concepts arose from reason alone, they would not have the practical and psychological effects that everyone agrees they have.

This argument too remains controversial. The first premise, like the second one, continues to generate considerable debate. Some philosophers think the first premise implies that moral concepts, when grasped, are inherently motivating or intrinsically action–guiding. The awareness that an action is right or obligatory by itself provides an agent with a motive to perform it, although the motive may not necessarily be sufficient to outweigh others that might also be present. If an agent perceives that an action is right, she necessarily has some motive to do it. If she does not have a motive, she has not perceived what her duty is.

Other philosophers question whether Hume is committed to the idea that moral perceptions are inherently motivating. Perhaps only his rationalist opponents are committed to this view. If we believe that Hume is committed to the idea that moral perceptions are intrinsically action–guiding, he must show that the moral sentiments are inherently motivating. If we accept that only rationalists are committed to the idea that moral ideas are intrinsically motivating, no such burden falls on him. Philosophers today are divided about whether moral concepts are intrinsically action–guiding. Those who favor this view think it captures our intuition that the morally good person is someone who does the right action because she sees it is right, rather than being prodded by sanctions. Others are comfortable denying that moral ideas are inherently motivating.

The argument from truth and falsehood

Hume's next argument, which has several sub-arguments, relies on the characterization of reason as concerned with discovering truth and falsehood. In one sub-argument, Hume explicitly mentions Wollaston. He pretends to interpret Wollaston as claiming that the criterion of immoral actions is the intention to cause false beliefs in others. But Wollaston's view is that immoral actions express falsehoods, not that they cause false beliefs.

Hume's misunderstanding of Wollaston's view, however, allows him to make fun of him, as his example makes clear. Someone walks by an exposed window and sees Hume cavorting with his neighbor's wife, and is thereby caused to falsely believe that she is his wife. He points out that the wrongdoing in this example is unintentional since his intention is to satisfy his lust, not to cause false beliefs in others. Furthermore, if he had taken the precaution of pulling the shades down, his actions would not have been immoral, since they would not have caused false beliefs in others.

Hume offers two criticisms of Wollaston's actual view that wrong actions express falsehoods. One is that he fails to explain the basis of immoral actions. All he has done is to reduce immorality to one kind—expressing a falsehood. But why is that morally wrong? His more important criticism is that Wollaston's criterion is circular. It is wrong for me to take your property without your permission because I falsely declare it to be mine, not yours. But if we ask why this is what my action means, the answer is that the fact that it is yours *means* that I should not steal it. In every case, the truth that is supposedly denied by a wrong action already has moral content. In one of the earliest reviews of Wollaston's theory, a critic raises the circularity problem, and since then, virtually everyone writing on him has as well.

The argument from relations of ideas or matters of fact

Hume's fourth argument is directed against Clarke, among others, and it depends on the characterization of reason as comparing ideas to find relations among them. If we were able to determine what is virtuous or vicious by means of reason alone, the basis of moral distinctions necessarily lies either in some a priori relation of ideas or in some matter of fact.

In his second *Enquiry* account, Hume reverses the way in which he proceeds in the *Treatise*. He first looks at the idea that the virtuousness or viciousness of an action consists in some matter of fact and then turns to the idea that it lies in some relation of ideas. This way of proceeding is better, since it sets up Clarke's view that morality lies in some a priori relation.

Hume's argument that virtue and vice do not lie in some matter of fact, as he presents it in the *Treatise*, is this:

> Take any action allow'd to be vicious: Wilful murder, for instance. Examine it in all lights, and see if you can find that matter of fact, or real existence, which you call *vice*. In which-ever way you take it, you find only certain passions, motives, volitions, and thoughts. There is no other matter of fact in the case. (T 3.1.1. 26)

Hume puts this point more clearly in the second *Enquiry*. He considers the "crime" of ingratitude. However, he points out that not being grateful is not bad in every situation. It is bad only when it is directed at someone who has been kind to you or has helped you. This means that the badness of being ungrateful cannot lie in any particular fact of the case. If it does not lie in any particular fact, perhaps it lies in some relation among the facts. So Hume considers Clarke's view that the moral badness of an action lies in some relation of ideas.

Hume argues that if you think that the virtuousness or viciousness of an action lies in one of the four a priori relations of ideas, "you run into absurdities" (T 3.1.1.19). These relations hold not only among human beings, but also among inanimate objects and non-human animals. Spruce trees and pine trees resemble each other and an elephant weighs more than a mouse. If these relations are found in inanimate objects and non-human animals, it should be just as appropriate to praise and blame them as it is to praise and blame us. However, everyone agrees that while we may be annoyed with animals and inanimate objects, we do not morally blame them.

In his second *Enquiry* discussion, Hume focuses on the possi-bility that vice rests on the relation of contrariety, a possibility he admits has some initial plausibility. Consider again a case of someone who acts ungratefully. Suppose I respond to your kindness with indifference or, even worse, by treating you badly. Since the relation of contrariety holds between my conduct and yours, we might be tempted to think that the viciousness of ingratitude lies in that relation. But if I respond to your meanness with indifference, or, even better, by helping you, there is the same relation of contrariety. Yet, in the first case, my conduct is blamable, while in the second, it is laudable. The relation of contrariety by itself does not tell us which actions are morally good actions and which are morally bad.

Clarke, however, never claimed that the virtuousness and viciousness of actions lies in one of Hume's relations of ideas, since he does not share the idea that reason consists in discerning these specific *four* relations. Nevertheless, he thinks that we arrive at moral ideas by means of reason alone. Since Hume's claim that there are four a priori relations of ideas is empirical, he cannot prove it conclusively. So he imagines that Clarke will reply by saying that he has overlooked an important relation—the 'ought' relation. Hume complains, however, that rationalists have never explained this new relation and he argues that they cannot explain it.

Hume offers a reductio of the rationalist idea that virtue and vice consists in some relation discoverable by reason alone, showing that it leads to absurd results. He looks at two of the most horrible crimes human beings are capable of committing, parricide and incest, and argues that any relation the rationalist might propose to account for these crimes will also be found among trees and animals. Everyone agrees that human beings may act immorally, but trees and animals cannot. If the same relations are found in cases involving human beings and in those involving trees and animals, but we only judge human beings as acting badly, then the viciousness of an action does not lie in a relation of ideas.

Hume's first example concerns an oak tree. When a sapling grows big enough to overtop and destroy its parent by blocking out the sunlight, no one thinks it has acted badly. The "parent" tree is the cause of the "child" tree and the "child" tree is the cause of destruction of the "parent" tree. Exactly the same relations are found in cases of human parricide. The human parent is the cause of the human child and the human child is the cause of the destruction of the human parent. Since the same relations are found in both cases, but we agree that only human beings can act immorally, the moral badness of parricide does not lie in any relation of ideas. Hume offers a similar argument about incest. When non-human animals have sexual relations with their siblings, we do not judge it to be morally bad, but when human beings have sex with their siblings we do, yet all the relations are the same in both cases.

The is–ought argument

Hume begins his final argument, the "Is–Ought" argument, by remarking that moral theorists typically first try to establish some factual claim, for example, that God exists, that human beings are naturally sociable, or that society is necessary if human beings are to preserve themselves. After a while, however, instead of finding propositions joined by "*is*, and *is not*," he encounters propositions joined by "an *ought*, or an *ought not*." He finds this troubling:

> For as this *ought*, or *ought not*, expresses some new relation … 'tis necessary that it shou'd be observ'd and explain'd; and at the same time that a reason shou'd be given, for what seems altogether inconceivable, how this new relation can be a deduction from others, which are entirely different from it. (T 3.1.1.27)

Notice that Hume is assuming that the "ought" relation cannot be basic in the sense of not needing to be explained in terms of some other relation. Thomas Reid (1710–96), one of Hume's rationalist successors, complained that Hume's criticism is therefore unfair, since even Hume must think that some relations are basic in this sense. For example, Hume takes the relation of resemblance to be basic. He does not try to explain it in terms of other relations and there is no other relation that could explain it. The rationalist may be thinking that the "ought" relation is basic in the same way.

Early twentieth-century philosophers thought the "Is–Ought" argument was pivotal. Many believed it supported the dictum that no "ought" can be legitimately derived from an "is," which in turn supported a non-cognitivist position in ethics. Non-cognitivism is the view that ethical judgments cannot be true or false, since they do not describe facts. While many maintained that this argument commits Hume to a non-cognitivist view of moral judgments, others point to passages they believe show that he was a cognitivist. Still others argue that Hume was not a player in this debate.

This concludes Hume's case against moral rationalism. In the next two chapters, we look at how he develops his version of sentimentalism.

9

Sympathy and the general point of view

Hume takes the defeat of rationalism to be the triumph of sentimentalism. He concludes that moral concepts spring from sentiment, not reason. As an empiricist, he claims that our ideas of moral goodness and badness are based in impressions, specifically, in the sentiments of approval and disapproval. Of course, he is not the first to argue that moral ideas arise from sentiments. Hutcheson maintains that we possess, in addition to our other senses, a special moral sense that disposes us to respond to benevolence with the distinctive feeling of approbation. Hume, however, rejects the idea that the moral sentiments arise from a sense that is "an *original* quality" and part of our "*primary* constitution" (T 3.1.2.6).

There are two reasons why Hume rejects the idea of an original moral sense. First, he believes that there are many different types of virtue, not all of which are types of benevolence, as Hutcheson claims. Respecting people's property rights, keeping promises, and obeying government are not reducible to benevolence. Nor are courage, industry, or perseverance, to mention just a few more virtues. Suppose we agree with Hume that there are many different sorts of virtues, but keep Hutcheson's idea of a moral sense. Hume thinks that we would then have to believe that we have many different "original instincts" or senses—one for each virtue—which dispose us to approve of each of them separately. Second, Hume complains that not only is the idea that we have multiple instincts implausible, but it is also contrary to the "usual maxims, by which nature is conducted, where a few principles produce all the variety we observe in the universe" (T 3.1.2.6). Instead of multiplying senses, we should look for a few general principles to explain our approval of the various virtues.

For Hume, however, the real problem with Hutcheson's version of sentimentalism is that he fails to provide a naturalistic explanation of the origins of the moral sentiments. Recall that he thinks a naturalistic explanation is one that is consistent with the scientific picture of the world and thus avoids appealing to anything supernatural. Hutcheson just claims—*hypothesizes*—that we possess a unique moral sense. If asked why we have a moral sense, his reply is simply that God implanted it in us.

Although in his *critical phase* Hume freely borrows many of Hutcheson's arguments to criticize moral rationalism, his rejection of the idea of a God-given moral sense puts him on a radically different path from Hutcheson in his *constructive phase*. One way of understanding Hume's project is to see it as an attempt to naturalize Hutcheson's moral sense theory. He aims to provide a wholly naturalistic explanation of how we come to experience the moral sentiments that also explains why we approve of the different virtues by reference to a few general principles. In the course of explaining the origin of the moral sentiments, Hutcheson's idea of an original moral sense disappears from Hume's account of morality.

In the first part of this chapter, we examine Hume's version of sentimentalism. In the second part, we look at his account of the natural virtues. He presents his naturalistic explanation of the moral sentiments in stages. In 3.1.2 of the *Treatise*, he tells us what kind of feelings the moral sentiments are. In 3.3.1, he raises an initial puzzle about the moral sentiments, which he solves by claiming that the moral sentiments arise from sympathy. His explanation of the moral sentiments in terms of sympathy allows him to explain how we come to have impersonal sentiments about others as opposed to self-interested sentiments. However, later on in the same section, Hume raises two objections to the idea that the moral sentiments spring from sympathy. He introduces the idea of the "general point of view" in response to these objections. The general point of view is one of the most innovative components of his explanation of the moral sentiments.

The moral sentiments

Hume often refers to the moral sentiments as feelings of approval and disapproval, but he also calls them feelings of praise and blame, esteem and contempt. According to him, we experience the moral sentiments when we take up the point of view of a spectator or judge and contemplate our own or other people's character traits from that perspective. He thinks it is obvious what kind of feelings the moral sentiments are. Approval is a kind of pleasant or agreeable feeling and disapproval is a kind of painful or disagreeable feeling. Appealing to experience in support of this claim, he remarks that a generous and just action strikes us as fair and beautiful, while the sight of cruelty and treachery is abhorrent to us. He adds,

> No enjoyment equals the satisfaction we receive from the company of those we love and esteem; as the greatest of all punishments is to be oblig'd to pass our lives with those we hate or contemn. (T 3.1.2.2)

Hume is not saying that we like associating with people who love us and dislike associating with people who hate us. Rather, he is saying that what is morally important to us are the character traits of the people with whom we interact on a daily basis. Virtue is what is lovable and estimable in people's characters and vice is what is unlovable and hateful in them.

In several passages, Hume describes moral approval and disapproval as calm kinds of love and hatred. Approval and disapproval are "nothing but a fainter and more imperceptible love or hatred" (T 3.3.5.1). When we evaluate our own character traits, love and hatred are replaced by pride and humility. As calm types of love and hatred, he thinks that the moral sentiments are distinguished from the more personal loves and hatreds we have for ourselves, our family, and our friends. According to him, our personal loves and hatreds are typically violent and biased. We love members of our family and friends more than others. They are also variable, differing from person to person—the individuals I love may not be the same individuals you love. In his explanation of the moral sentiments, Hume starts with our more violent, biased, and variable personal loves and hatreds and then shows how they become calm, impartial, and stable.

On Hume's view, the moral sentiments are the source of moral value. They are what make character traits and motives morally good or bad. As he says,

> To have a sense of virtue, is nothing but to *feel* a satisfaction of a particular kind from the contemplation of a character. The very *feeling* constitutes our praise or admiration... We do not infer a character to be virtuous, because it pleases: But in feeling that it pleases ... we in effect feel that it is virtuous. (T 3.1.2.3)

We do not judge character traits and motives as morally good because they are inherently virtuous. They are morally good only because we approve of them.

One way to understand Hume's point is by comparing moral value with what modern philosophers say about secondary qualities. According to these philosophers, secondary qualities—such as color—are "subjective." They are not properties of objects. Objects have color only because of the way that they affect us. Similarly, Hume believes that character traits and motives have moral value only because of the way they affect us. Without the reflective sentiments of approval and disapproval, there would be no such thing as moral value.

Although there would be no such thing as moral value unless we were able to feel approval, Hume explains why *we think* that character traits and motives have inherent value. His explanation is similar to the one the moderns give for why we think objects are colored. Because we have a propensity to project color onto objects, we come to think of color as a property inherent in objects themselves. Similarly, because we have a propensity to project our approval onto people's character traits and motives, we come to think of virtue as a property inherent in them and to regard our approval as a response to that property. Nevertheless, character traits and motives are virtuous only because we approve of them.

Hume, like Hutcheson, assumes that in the first instance we morally judge people's character traits and motives rather than their outward actions. When we praise actions, we consider them as "signs or indications" of the character traits and inner motives that produced them (T 3.2.1.2; T 3.3.1.4). When you act humanely—comforting the sick, relieving the suffering of the distressed, or giving to the poor—it is your inner motive of humanity that is morally good. Your actions are good only because they are expressive of good motives.

Hume identifies both what has value and what makes things valuable with features of our psychology. First-order sentiments and passions have moral value and second-order sentiments are what give them value. On Hume's sentimentalist picture, morality is entirely a product of human nature.

Sympathy and impersonal sentiments

Having identified the moral sentiments, Hume turns to his naturalistic explanation of how they arise. He wants "to discover the true origin of morals, and of that love and hatred, which arises" when we contemplate our own or other people's character traits and motives (T 3.3.1.6). In this stage of his explanation, Hume shows how we come to have impersonal sentiments about others as opposed to self-interested sentiments.

He begins with a puzzle. Suppose you see a bully beating up a vulnerable victim, and both the bully and victim are not related or connected to you in any way. Hume believes that the victim's pain will cause you to hate the bully and that you will judge his cruelty to be morally bad. But why should we be pleased or displeased by things that involve the welfare of people we don't know or otherwise care about? Why should we care about what happens to strangers?

Hume thinks that the clue to solving this puzzle is to be found in the same principle of human nature that he invokes in his explanation of how we arrive at causal beliefs—namely, that the principles of association not only relate perceptions, but also transmit force and vivacity from one perception to another, as we saw in Chapter 5. He believes that the transfer of vivacity also explains what he calls *sympathy*, which is the basis of moral approval and disapproval.

Sympathy, for Hume, is one of the most important psychological mechanisms. It explains how the feelings, sentiments, and even beliefs of one person are transferred to another person. Sympathy is not itself a passion or feeling. Sometimes we use the term "sympathy" to mean the pity or compassion we feel for someone's suffering, but Hume is not using it this way. In fact, he explains pity and compassion by appealing to sympathy. Sympathy also is not a motive. Although sympathy explains how I come to experience your pain, it does not determine my response to it. My pain may move me to help you or to take an aspirin. Sympathy, for Hume, is a mechanism that explains how we come to feel what others are feeling. His initial and most detailed explanation of sympathy is in *Treatise* 2.1.11.

Hume thinks sympathy is at work in everyday cases such as these: When your friend is miserable, so are you. When you walk into a room full of cheerful people, you feel cheerful. When an actor in a movie you are watching is terrified, you feel terrified. In all these cases, we come to feel what others are feeling. We enter into their feelings by having these feelings ourselves. Sympathy is a process that moves us from an idea of what someone is feeling to having the feeling ourselves. There are four steps to this process.

First, you figure out what someone is feeling or, in some cases, what she would be feeling if she understood the situation she is in. We do this in various ways. Sometimes people tell us what they are feeling. If they do not tell us, we must infer what they are feeling, since we cannot directly inspect their feelings. By observing the effects of people's passions—their bodily gestures, verbal behaviors, and actions—we are able to figure out what they are feeling. We rely on our own experiences to help determine which bodily expressions, verbal behaviors, and actions are caused by which passions. When someone blushes, we infer that he is embarrassed, because we blush when we are embarrassed. Alternatively, we may witness the causes of people's passions and infer what they are feeling or would be feeling. When we see the instruments laid out for surgery, we understand that the individual about to undergo surgery would be anxious if he saw these instruments.

Second, appealing to the associative principle of *resemblance*, Hume says you are aware that the other person resembles you. Every human being resembles every other human being to some extent. We tend to experience similar sorts of passions in similar situations and express them in similar ways. People feel angry when insulted, sad when a family member dies, and anxious before taking an important test. But we also resemble some people more than others, for example, those who share our language, interests, and culture, and are the same age. Hume thinks that the other two associative principles—*contiguity* and *causality*—also operate in the production of sympathy, relating individuals who are located closely to us in time or space, or who are family members or teachers.

Third, Hume claims that we always have a forceful, lively, and vivacious impression of ourselves. Fourth, he appeals to the same principle of human nature he uses in his explanation of causal belief. The principles of association not only relate two perceptions, but also transmit force and vivacity from one perception to another.

Here is how sympathy works: You first form an idea of what someone is feeling. Suppose your friend recently suffered a devastating loss. You realize she is sad. You are also aware of the resemblances between your friend and yourself, so that principle of association links you. The associative principle of resemblance transmits the force and vivacity from the impression you have of yourself to the idea of your friend's sadness, with the result that your idea of your friend's sadness becomes enlivened. Now recall a point Hume made early on: the difference between an impression and an idea is that the former is more lively and vivacious. He thinks that if an idea of a passion is sufficiently lively and vivacious, it becomes the very passion itself. You now feel sad too, but not quite so strongly as your friend.

The way Hume uses the idea that the associative principles transmit force and vivacity in his explanation of sympathy is similar to the way he uses it in his explanation of causal inference. If we have an impression of an effect (smoke), the associative principles give rise not only to the idea of its cause (fire), but they also transmit some of its force and vivacity to the idea of its cause. As a result, we come to believe that there is fire in the vicinity. A belief is an idea that is so lively that it is *like* an impression, and influences us in the way impressions do. In a similar way, our ideas of the passions of others are enlivened by their association with the lively idea of ourselves. But the result in the case of sympathy is even stronger, since if an idea of a passion is sufficiently enlivened it becomes the very passion itself.

Hume appeals to sympathy to explain a wide range of phenomena. He thinks it explains our interest in history and current affairs, our ability to enjoy literature, paintings, movies, and other artistic endeavors. More generally, it explains our sociability—our deep desire to live with others. It is central to his explanation of our particular passions, our aesthetic judgments, and, more importantly for our purposes, our moral judgments.

Sympathy, on Hume's view, enables us to have impersonal as opposed to self-interested sentiments about anyone, even about strangers. When we see the bully beating up the vulnerable victim, we respond sympathetically to the victim's pain, even though both the bully and victim are strangers. Causal reasoning focuses our attention on the bully, since he is the cause of the victim's pain with which we sympathize, and we end up hating him. We hate the bully's cruelty not because of the pain it causes us, but because we sympathize with the pain it inflicts on the victim. In this case, we have an impersonal sentiment about one stranger, the bully, on behalf of another stranger, the victim. The impersonal hatred we experience in this case is different from the personal hatred we would feel if the bully were cruel to us.

In a similar way, we may love someone because of her generous aid to victims of a natural disaster, even though both she and the victims are strangers. Our sympathy with the victims makes us share in the pleasures that the generous person brings them. We focus our attention on the generous person since she is the cause of the victims' pleasures with which we sympathize, and we end up loving her. Once again, the impersonal love we experience in this case is different from the personal love we would feel if she were generous to us. Sympathy makes us interested in the concerns of others and explains how we are able to have impersonal feelings about them, without turning their interests into ours.

Although there is one more stage to Hume's explanation of the moral sentiments, we are already in a position to see some advantages his explanation in terms of sympathy has over Hutcheson's hypothesis of a God-given moral sense. One is that it provides a unified theory of the mind. Hume explains our moral sentiments by appealing to deep-seated principles he has already uncovered in his examination of the mind. He explains sympathy by appealing to the same associative principles that he invokes to explain causal beliefs. Without sympathy, and the associative principles that explain it, we would be unimaginably different than we are—creatures who lack casual and moral ideas.

The general point of view

Although sympathy explains why we are able to have impersonal feelings of love and hatred, Hume does not think his explanation of the moral sentiments is complete. In the next part of his explanation, he raises two objections he imagines opponents would make to his claim that the moral sentiments arise from sympathy.

The first objection is the "sympathy is variable" objection (T 3.3.1.14). Sympathy enables us to enter into the feelings of anyone because we resemble everyone to some extent. But it is an essential feature of Hume's account of the natural and spontaneous operation of sympathy that our ability to respond sympathetically varies with variations in the associative relations. I am able to sympathize more easily and strongly with someone who resembles me or is related to me by contiguity or causation. The more someone resembles me in character, language, occupation, hobbies, sex, and so on, the stronger the sympathy. Disasters that occur in our own lifetime are felt more keenly than those that occurred in the distant past. We feel the pain and suffering of our children more easily and strongly than the pain and suffering of others. For shorthand, call the natural and spontaneous operation of sympathy "unregulated" sympathy.

Although unregulated sympathy explains how we can experience impersonal feelings of love and hatred, these feelings too vary with variations in the associative principles. However, like many of his contemporaries, Hume believes that there is general agreement about the content of morality. We morally love and hate the same sorts of character traits and motives, regardless of whether the person speaks the same language we do, is in the same profession, lives in the same town, or is a relative or friend. The objection, then, is that moral approval can't be based in sympathy because our moral approvals do not vary, but the loves and hatreds that result from "unregulated" sympathy do vary.

The second objection is that "virtue in rags" still evokes our approval. On Hume's explanation of sympathy, we sympathize with the actual effects of a person's character traits. We praise someone's kindness because we sympathize with the benefits it bestows on her associates. We praise someone's industriousness because we sympathize with the benefits it confers on herself and her co-workers. However, misfortune, accidents, or lack of opportunity may prevent an individual from exercising her good character traits. A charitable person may be too poor to have anything to give. In cases such as this, the beneficial effects of these traits will not be realized and, as a result, there will be nothing with which to sympathize. Nevertheless,

> Virtue in rags is still virtue; and the love, which it procures, attends a man into a dungeon or desert, where the virtue can no longer be exerted in action, and is lost to all the world. (T 3.3.1.19)

We still love a generous and kind person, even if she is stranded on a desert island where there is no opportunity to act generously.

Hume responds by claiming that moral love and hatred arise from the sympathy we feel when we regulate our sympathetic responses by taking up what he calls a "steady" or "general" point of view (T 3.3.1.15). There are two regulative features of the general point of view. First, we survey a person's character from the perspective of that person's narrow circle—the individuals with whom she regularly interacts. Typically, these will include the person herself and her family, friends, neighbors, co-workers, and so on. We sympathize with all the people who make up a person's narrow circle, and we judge character traits to be virtuous or vicious in terms of whether they are good or bad for everyone in her narrow circle. Second, we further regulate sympathy by relying on general rules that specify the usual effects and tendencies of character traits, rather than their actual effects. If misfortune prevents a person from exercising her benevolent impulses, we judge her benevolence to be morally good because in normal circumstances it would be beneficial to others.

By putting together the two regulatory features, we arrive at the general point of view. The regulative features define a perspective we can share with everyone, from which we may survey a person's character traits. When we occupy the general point of view, we sympathize with the person herself and her usual associates, and we come to love that person for character traits that are normally useful and pleasant for herself and her associates.

The general point of view is the moral perspective. On Hume's view, we do not experience the moral sentiments or have moral concepts unless we have already taken up the general point of view and regulated our sympathetic loves and hatreds. The moral sentiments and the moral concepts to which they give rise are *products* of having taken up the general point of view.

The moral evaluations that result when we take up the general point of view differ in important ways from the loves and hatreds that arise from two other perspectives—the perspective of self-interest and the perspective of unregulated sympathy. From a self-interested perspective, I like anyone who benefits me, and dislike anyone who harms me. I dislike my rival's industriousness because it counteracts my own interests. But by viewing my rival through the eyes of her narrow circle and sympathizing with the effects her character trait would typically have on them, I come to see her industriousness as morally loveable.

Similarly, what we love and hate from the perspective of unregulated sympathy may be opposed to our moral loves and hatreds. From the perspective of unregulated sympathy, it is easier for me to sympathize with people who resemble me or are contiguous or causally related to me in specific ways. Someone whose generosity benefits people from my hometown will arouse a stronger love in me than someone whose generosity benefits those who live in a far away city. But by viewing the latter person's generosity through the eyes of her own narrow circle and sympathizing with the beneficial effects her generosity would normally have on them, I come to see her generosity as morally lovable.

The general point of view, with its regulation of sympathy, brings a kind of impartiality to our moral judgments. The regulation of sympathy ensures that we put aside not only self-interested considerations, but also considerations derived from the special ways in which we are related to others. In judging others, we discount the fact that they are rivals, resemble us in special ways, live nearby, or are family members.

The regulation of sympathy also makes our moral judgments more stable and regular, explaining why we tend to agree about which traits are morally good and which are morally bad. Approval and disapproval are calm forms of love and hatred that arise when we survey people from a common perspective—we all look at the person through the eyes of the person's narrow circle, sympathizing with the usual effects and tendencies of her character traits. As calm forms of love and hatred, the moral sentiments are distinct not only from our more personal and violent loves and hatreds, but also from our impersonal but variable loves and hatreds that arise from unregulated sympathy. Hume begins his explanation of the moral sentiments with our more personal, variable, and violent loves and hatreds—feelings that are not themselves moral—and then he describes the process whereby we transform them into moral loves and hatreds. The effect of taking up the general point of view and regulating our sympathetic responses is to make these violent, variable, and irregular loves and hatreds calm, stable, and regular.

The virtues as pleasant and useful attributes

Hume argues that when we take up the general point of view, we approve of four types of virtue: character traits that are immediately agreeable to the possessor, useful to the possessor, immediately agreeable to others, or useful to others. He appeals to experience to support this conclusion.

Hume thinks that the character traits that are useful to others or to society as a whole are the most important type of virtue. Benevolence and the other social virtues, such as being sociable, humane, grateful, friendly, and generous, are qualities that help us to promote the good of others and make us proper members of society. Respecting property rights, keeping promises, and upholding contracts are traits that are useful to society as a whole. Character traits that are useful to the possessor help to achieve her projects and plans and include such traits as prudence, temperance, perseverance, strength of mind, and frugality.

Some character traits are immediately agreeable—pleasant—to others or to their possessors. We value them for their agreeableness rather than their utility. Character traits that are immediately agreeable to others include being witty, well mannered, modest, and clean. Hume calls these the "companionable" virtues since they make us good companions, someone with whom people want to associate. Character traits that are immediately agreeable to their possessors keep us in good humor with ourselves and include such traits as cheerfulness, composure, and contentment.

The four types of virtue are not mutually exclusive; we may approve of some character traits on more than one ground. We praise benevolence primarily because it is useful to others, yet since it is a "sweet, smooth, tender, and agreeable" feeling, we also praise it because it is immediately agreeable to its possessor (EPM 9. 2. 21). We approve of cheerfulness because it is immediately pleasant not only to those who possess it, but also to their friends and companions.

Hume realizes that some character traits may be used for good or bad purposes. Consequently, they need to be regulated by other character traits in order to be virtuous. For example, "courage and ambition when not regulated by benevolence, are fit only to make a tyrant and public robber" (T 3.3.3.3). Similarly, a person may use his intelligence or perseverance in the service of a bad purpose— say, eliminating a rival by slandering him—so these too need to be governed by benevolence and justice to be morally good.

Against self-interest theories of approval

In the second *Enquiry,* Hume uses his fourfold classification of the virtues to drive home his claim that the moral sentiments spring from sympathy, arguing that they do not spring from self-interest. As we noted in Chapter 8, although he continues to oppose the moral rationalists in the second *Enquiry,* his main opponents are the self-interest theorists, Hobbes and Mandeville. Hume follows Hutcheson in assuming that they were offering a rival theory of approval and disapproval. On his understanding of them, we approve of people when they benefit us and disapprove of them when they harm us. Approval and disapproval are based in self-interested considerations.

Hume is confident that "the voice of nature and experience" shows that the self-interest theory, understood in this way, is mistaken. If our approval and disapproval were based on thoughts about the possible advantages and disadvantages of actions to us, we would never feel approval and disapproval of people from "very distant ages and remote countries," since they cannot possibly help or hurt us (EPM 5.1.7). We would never admire the good deeds of our enemies or rivals, since they are hurtful to us. We would also never approve or disapprove of characters portrayed in novels or movies, since they cannot possibly help or harm us.

Hume examines each of the four types of virtue in turn and argues that in each case, our approval is based in sympathy, not self-interest.

In Section 2 of the second *Enquiry*, he looks at the social virtues, benevolence, generosity, and charity: character traits that prompt us to help others, and in Section 5 he raises the kind of puzzle about moral evaluations, which we discussed earlier in this chapter. We find a person's generosity pleasing and agreeable, but generosity is a means to an end—the end is that the recipients are benefitted. If we find the means pleasing, the end must also be pleasing and agreeable. However, we approve of the generosity of others even when we are not benefitted. Why should we care about their generosity when it does not benefit us? We care because of sympathy. We approve of the social virtues not because they benefit us, but because we sympathize with the benefits they bestow on others.

A similar argument applies to the remaining three types of virtue. In Section 6 of the second *Enquiry*, Hume asks why we approve of industriousness and good judgment, character traits that primarily benefit the person who has them. In most cases they are of absolutely no benefit to us and, in cases of rivalry, they counteract our interests. In Section 7, he looks at character traits such as cheerfulness, which are valued for their immediate agreeableness to the possessor. He points out that, in most cases, since we do not know the person, these traits are of no advantage to us, and yet we still approve of them. In Section 8, he argues that we approve of the companionable virtues, even if we are unacquainted with the person who has them. In all of these cases, we morally approve of the character traits not because they are advantageous to us, but because we sympathize with the advantages they confer on others. "All suspicion, therefore, of selfish regards, is here totally excluded" (EPM 6.3). Hume takes this as further evidence against the self-interest explanation and in support of his sympathy-based explanation.

The natural virtues

Hume contrasts the natural virtues with the artificial virtues, which arise from social practices we establish. He thinks that we are by nature benevolent creatures and are disposed to help others. Parents naturally love their children and are moved to care for them. We naturally care about ourselves and are moved to do things that further our own good. Hume discusses the natural virtues in *Treatise* 3.3.2-3 and in Sections 2, 6–8 of the second *Enquiry*.

Hume's conception of the natural virtues is opposed to the religiously-based conceptions of his day, as is his picture of human nature. According to him, one distinctive, but unhealthy, feature of modern moral philosophy, as opposed to that of the ancients, is that it unites moral theory with theology, bending it to the interests of religion. One way Hume signals his disdain for religiously-based moral theories is that he refuses to take his catalogue of virtues from *The Whole Duty of Man*, a devotional tract widely used in his time, which details our duties to God, others, and ourselves. Instead, his catalogue comes from the *Offices* of Cicero (103–43 BCE), the ancient Roman philosopher.

Hume rejects not only conservative and often harsh Christian conceptions of virtue, but also more benign Christian conceptions that philosophers like Hutcheson defended. The Scottish Presbyterian conception of virtue in which Hume was raised stressed the total corruption of fallen human nature. By eating the forbidden fruit, Adam broke his covenant with God, and consequently human beings are born not only ignorant of what they ought to do, but too weak-willed to do what they ought. Only a select few have the promise of a good afterlife. Humility, self-denial, privation, and suffering are core virtues.

Hutcheson's conception of virtue, with its emphasis on love, provides a kind of antidote to the harsh Scottish Presbyterian conception. He conceives of the deliverances of the moral sense as being a distinctive sort of love. What the moral sense loves most is the Christian love that aims at promoting the good of everyone. Although morality, on this view, is essentially a matter of love, this conception is too saccharine for Hume. In fact, he denies that there is such a thing as calm universal benevolence that aims at the good of humankind. He argues that benevolence, generosity, charity, and other social affections are always directed towards specific individuals or groups of people. There must be something special about them or our relation to them that motivates us to provide assistance.

Hume is convinced that we would be morally better and happier without conceptions of virtue based on Christian doctrines. He uses his fourfold classification of the virtues to make several changes to the Christian catalogue of virtues. Christianity, he says, is the only religion to rank humility as a virtue and pride a vice, but in the "judgment of the world" well-grounded pride has always been admired. Reversing humility and pride, he makes humility a vice and pride a virtue. By pride, he means a kind of proper self-evaluation that is based on an accurate assessment of our characters. Being proud in this sense gives us confidence in carrying out our projects and plans.

Hume goes even further and throws out the "whole train of monkish virtues," arguing that "celibacy, fasting, penance, mortification, self-denial, humility, silence, [and] solitude" are not real virtues. The natural virtues consist in character traits that are useful or immediately agreeable to ourselves or to others, but the "monkish" virtues are neither pleasing nor useful to anyone. They

> neither advance a man's fortune in the world, nor render him a more valuable member of society; neither qualify him for the entertainment of company, nor encrease his power of self-enjoyment. (EPM 9.1.3)

So, Hume transfers the monkish virtues "to the opposite column" and places them in the "catalogue of vices" (EPM 9.1.3). The so-called virtues the monkish theorist recommends are alienating, life-denying, and anti-social.

Another change Hume makes to the catalogue of natural virtues is that he treats natural talents as being on the same footing as the virtues. Natural talents are the mental abilities people are born with that give them a head start in life. Just as some people are born with certain physical endowments—they are naturally more beautiful, graceful, or athletic—some people are born with more raw intelligence, good sense, or eloquence. In both *Treatise* 3.3.4 and *Appendix* 4 of the second *Enquiry*, Hume argues that the debate about whether natural talents are moral virtues is, like the free-will debate, only a verbal dispute. In common life, people value their intellectual talents as much as their moral virtues. No one likes being called a fool, dim-witted, or indecisive. We would never say, except ironically, that someone was a person of great virtue, but was an "egregious blockhead" (EPM Appendix 4.2).

Hume's quarrel is with clerics, educators, moralists, and other reformers of his day who want to change us—or, at least, our outward behavior—to make us morally better, when understood in Christian terms. He remarks that the distinction between moral virtues and natural talents is a modern invention and it is no accident that it arose from moral theories based in theological considerations. Ancient moralists whose theories were independent of theology did not think it necessary to distinguish moral virtues from natural talents.

Modern moral philosophers, or more accurately, "divines under the disguise of philosophers," defend the distinction between moral virtues and natural abilities by arguing that the moral virtues are voluntary and arise from free will, whereas natural talents are involuntary (EPM Appendix 4.21). But Hume has already argued that there is no such thing as free will in the sense that these reformers attach to the term—liberty of indifference. Actions that spring from the traditional virtues and those that spring from the natural abilities are caused. To say that an action is voluntary is to say that it is not coerced. Moreover, he argues that character traits that evoke pleasure in onlookers are virtuous and since involuntary character traits cause pleasure, they too should count as virtuous. An individual's kindness excites pleasure in onlookers, but so does someone's intelligence or sparkling wit. Why not include them in the list of virtues?

Finally, Hume argues that since our sympathetic reactions are guided by what is normal and natural in human nature, we approve of what is normal and natural for human beings. Sympathy makes us feel sorry for a child who is neglected by her parents and, as a result, we disapprove of them. This is because parents normally take care of their children. It is also normal for us to love our children better than our nephews, nephews better than strangers, where everything else is equal. Sympathy makes us approve of this sort of partiality, judging it to be morally good (T 3.2.1.18).

On Hume's conception of the natural virtues, what we approve of are certain natural motives and affections. It follows that the morally best person acts from these natural and spontaneous affections rather than from the motive of duty—performing the morally good action because he sees that it is morally good. A father who cares for his child because he is moved by his spontaneous love for his child acts from the best sort of motive. Someone who happens to lack a feeling human beings normally have, but manages to do the right thing, may perform the action from a "certain sense of duty" (T 3.2.1.8). With respect to the natural virtues, the motive of duty functions to fill in gaps left by nature. The motive of duty in these sorts of cases is second rate.

   The fact that Hume thinks the social virtues are the most important type of virtue reflects his belief that we are by nature deeply social creatures. Not only do we have an "ardent desire of society," we are also the most "fitted for it" (T 2.2.5.15). When we judge someone to be morally good, we typically list the character traits that make him a "safe companion, an easy friend, a gentle master, an agreeable husband, or an indulgent father" (T 3.3.3.9). We arrive at the ideal of the morally good person—someone who has the natural virtues—by imagining the person in a wide variety of roles and relationships—mother, friend, fellow-worker, and neighbor—and rely on general rules that specify which character traits normally have good effects on others. The conception that results is a picture of human beings as essentially social creatures—good parents, siblings, friends, neighbors, and fellow-workers—those who are good in all of the roles and relationships they occupy. He concludes that the ultimate test of "merit and virtue" is this:

> if there be no relation in life, in which I cou'd not wish to stand to a particular person, his character must so far be allow'd to be perfect. If he be as little wanting to himself as to others, his character is entirely perfect. (T 3.3.3.9)

Although, for Hume, the social virtues are especially important, self-regarding virtues are also valuable in their own right. To be morally good, you must not only be useful and pleasant to others, but also useful and pleasant to yourself.

   Hume's model of virtue, which he describes in the "Conclusion" to the second *Enquiry*, is a young man by the name of Cleanthes who is about to be married. Hume imagines his friends and associates congratulating the prospective father-in-law on such a happy prospect for his daughter. The first person remarks that anyone who has dealings with the young man is sure of benevolent and fair treatment (useful to others). The second person, presumably a lawyer or businessman, admires Cleanthes' abilities, which promise success in the legal and commercial worlds (useful to the possessor). The third person met Cleanthes at a party where he was its "life and soul"—witty, gallant, and well mannered (agreeable to others). The fourth person, Cleanthes' close friend, adds that his cheerfulness pervades his whole life, enabling him to meet misfortune and dangers with tranquility and serenity (agreeable to the possessor). As a model of "perfect" virtue, Cleanthes may seem rather slick to us (EPM 9.1.2).

Virtue and happiness

In the second *Enquiry*, Hume makes explicit what was implicit in his *Treatise* account of morality, arguing that his conception of the natural virtues, as opposed to Christian conceptions, offers us a pleasant and agreeable life here and now in this world. On his account

> The dismal dress falls off, with which many divines, and some philosophers have covered her; and nothing appears but gentleness, humanity, beneficence, affability ... She talks not of useless austerities and rigours, suffering and self-denial. She declares that her sole purpose is, to make ... all mankind, during every instant of their existence, if possible, cheerful and happy. (EPM 9.2.15)

It is easy to see how we would have a pleasant and agreeable life if we lived up to Hume's ideal of virtue. Having character traits that are useful and pleasant to ourselves obviously would make us happy. Without them, we would find ourselves constantly in trouble with few resources to overcome them. Having the companionable virtues—good manners, wit, and gentleness—will make us happy, since people will want to associate with us, something we desire as social creatures. The social virtues—benevolence, generosity, and kindness—are "sweet, smooth, tender, and agreeable" in themselves (EPM 9. 2. 21). In addition, others will love us for our kindness, and we will love ourselves knowing that we have done our part to help others. Having the natural virtues makes us happy.

Although Hume's conception of the good person is of someone who is completely loveable, good to other people and to herself, it is not very exacting. It does not demand that we should always be impartial in our interactions with other people. Our sympathetic responses are guided by what is normal and natural in human nature, and it is normal and natural for human beings to care more for their family members and friends than others. His conception does not imply that our nature needs to be tamed in order for us to live together peacefully, as Mandeville maintains. On Hume's view, we are by nature social creatures, especially suited for social life. Nor does his conception imply, as religious conceptions do, that human nature is corrupt, in need of salvation. According to Hume's conception, when we take up the general point of view, we find that human nature is fine—loveable pretty much as it is.

10

Justice

In this chapter, we look at Hume's constructive account of justice. Many of us think of justice as concerned with protecting people's liberties or distributing goods fairly, but Hume's conception is much narrower. Justice for him is concerned with establishing and maintaining property rights. If I own something—a car or computer—others have a duty to keep their hands off it, unless I give them permission to use it or give it to them.

Hume distinguishes justice as a *scheme* from justice as a *virtue*. One of his lasting insights is his realization that justice as a scheme is a *practice*, as the twentieth-century moral and political philosopher John Rawls (1921–2002) calls it (TJ 2.10.1–4). A practice is constituted by a set of rules. These rules, in turn, make certain actions possible. In baseball, for instance, there is no such thing as *striking out* unless there is some rule like "three strikes and you are out." Similarly, there is no such thing as *theft* unless there are rules that establish property rights. While it is possible for a practice to exist if its rules are violated some of the time, if they are universally violated, the practice ceases to exist. The practice itself, and the actions falling under it, depend upon the fact that people generally acknowledge and follow the rules of the practice. By contrast, justice as a *virtue* refers to a person's disposition to obey the rules of justice. We approve of this disposition, judging it to be morally good.

As with his explanation of the moral sentiments, Hume develops his account of justice in stages. First, he argues that justice is *artificial*. In saying this, he does not mean that justice is fake or unreal. He means that justice is a *practice* that we bring about because it is in our interest to do so. Establishing the practice requires intelligence and intention on our part, although he believes that the practice develops gradually over time as we come to experience the advantages of having it in place. He also means that justice as a *virtue*—the disposition to comply with the rules of justice—comes into existence only as the practice of justice develops.

In the next stage, Hume asks and answers two different questions. His first question concerns the origin of justice. What motivates human beings to institute a system of property rights? His aim here as elsewhere is to provide a naturalistic explanation, in this case of how the practice of justice develops. His second question is why we approve of individuals who obey the rules of justice and disapprove of those who disobey them. Interestingly, Hume agrees in outline—although not in detail—with Hobbes' answer to the first question. Both conceive of justice as the solution to problems human beings naturally face. Both argue that it is in our interest to have the practice of justice in place. However, he parts company with Hobbes when he answers his second question about why we approve of justice.

In the final stage, Hume raises a serious problem with his account of justice, one that also worried Hobbes. The problem concerns a sensible knave, as Hume calls him, or a free rider, as we would call him now. A free rider is someone who wants to reap the benefits of having a practice in place without having to follow its rules. For example, he wants to enjoy the benefits of a public park without paying taxes to support it.

Hume's explanation of justice is in 3.2.1 and 3.2.2 of the *Treatise* and also in Sections 3–4 and Appendix 3 of the second *Enquiry*. He raises the problem with his account of justice only in Part 2 of the "Conclusion" to the second *Enquiry*. Since his account of justice in the *Treatise* is more thorough, we follow it, supplementing it at points with material from the second *Enquiry*.

Before turning to Hume's account of justice, we should mention one preliminary point. He believes that we enter into a series of conventions, each of which is a solution to a problem. Each convention gives rise to new problems that in turn pressure us to establish new conventions. Justice is only the first of several conventions into which we enter. After justice is established, Hume thinks we develop conventions about transferring property and making promises and contracts. According to him, we are by nature cooperators, although at first we cooperate only with members of our own family. But it is also advantageous for us to cooperate with strangers, since it allows us to produce more goods and to exchange them. All three conventions are prior to the formation of government. On Hume's view, it is possible for a peaceful society of property owners who transfer and exchange material possessions to exist before there is government.

Justice is artificial

Philosophical context: the motive of duty

In *Treatise* 3.2.1, Hume argues that justice is artificial. He begins with an argument, sometimes called the *circle argument*, which concerns the motive or "sense" of duty. The motive of duty is doing the right thing because we see that it is right or doing the right thing because we think we ought to do it. When we ask people why they pay their debts, keep their promises, or refrain from stealing other people's possessions, they typically respond by saying, "It's the right thing to do." This thought motivated them to act as they did.

The circle argument is one of Hume's strongest arguments against moral rationalism. It is directed against the rationalist idea that the morally good person acts from the motive of duty, which both Clarke and Wollaston endorse. The argument appears here in the context of Hume's discussion of justice, rather than with his other arguments against moral rationalism, because the motive of duty seems to be the appropriate sort of motive for performing just actions, as we will see in a moment. However, he argues that doing your duty because you see it is your duty cannot be the *first* or *original* motive for doing your duty. To appreciate what is at stake in this argument, we first say something about the debate Hume inherits concerning the motive of duty, a debate that still continues to engage philosophers.

One way of understanding this debate is to ask yourself when you think the motive of duty is appropriate and when you think it is inappropriate. Suppose your friend takes you to the hospital for an outpatient operation. After she takes you home and settles you in, you thank her for everything she has done. She replies, "Of course I helped you; it's my duty to help my friends." This response seems out of place. It may even make you wonder whether your friend is really a friend. In cases like this, where there are ties of affection and friendship, we think people should be motivated by their natural and spontaneous feelings of love and friendship, not by the thought that it is their duty to help others. Helping your relatives and friends because you think it is your duty seems the wrong sort of motive for acts of benevolence, charity, generosity, and friendship.

Now consider another example. You loan someone some money, and when she repays you, you thank her. She then replies, "Oh, I'm glad to give you this money. I know you need it, so it would be stingy and ungenerous of me to keep it." This response also strikes us as inappropriate. Repaying a loan is not a matter of being generous or nice. It is something that is owed to you. You have a right to the money and the borrower has a duty to repay it. Since it is the borrower's duty to repay the loan, we think she should have been motivated by the thought that it is her duty to repay it, not by the thought that it would be generous or kind of her to do so. The motive of duty seems to be the appropriate sort of motive for acts of justice, keeping promises, and obeying the laws of our country.

Moral rationalists such as Clarke and Wollaston believe that the motive of duty is primary and should always be our motive. It should motivate us not only to keep our hands off other people's property and to keep promises, but also to care for our children, to help our friends, and to give to charity. When we care for and help people, we should be motivated by the thought that it is our duty to do so. In contrast, Hutcheson, as a sentimentalist, thinks that benevolence is primary and should operate in all cases. It should prompt us not only to help others and to be kind and generous to them, but also to repay loans, respect the property rights of others, and fulfill the terms of contracts. When we repay loans and keep promises, we should be motivated by feelings of love and generosity.

Hume's response to this debate is ingenious. By combining rationalist and sentimentalist insights, he makes room for both types of motives. According to him, parents should take care of their children and friends should help each other because they are motivated by feelings of love and affection. In cases like these, natural and spontaneous motives are morally best and should be primary. Hume argues, however, that in large and complex societies the standard motive for acting justly, repaying loans, and keeping promises is the motive of duty. It is the more stable motive and also the morally best motive—the motive we approve of the most. One of Hume's achievements is that he finds a place for the motive of duty within a sentimentalist framework.

The circle argument

It is not initially obvious, however, that Hume is going to claim that the motive of duty is the most stable and morally best motive for acting justly. This is because he begins by arguing that the motive of duty cannot be the *first* and *original* motive for performing just actions. As with many of his other arguments, he couches the circle argument in terms of virtues rather than duties.

Hume's first premise makes a point we mentioned in Chapter 9. When we praise actions, judging them to be morally good, we consider them as "signs or indications" of the inner motives that produced them. "Virtuous actions," he says, "derive their merit only from virtuous motives" (T 3.2.1.4). To use one of his examples, we judge actions such as comforting the sick, relieving the suffering of the distressed, and giving to the poor as morally good. Why? Because they are "proofs" of the person's inner motives—her humanity (T 3.2.1.6). We approve of her actions because we approve of the inner motive that produced them.

If the first premise is correct, it follows, Hume says, that the first or original motive "which bestows a merit on any action" cannot be "a regard to the virtue of that action". To think this motive is the first or original motive "is to reason in a circle":

> Before we can have such a regard, the action must be really virtuous; and this virtue must be deriv'd from some virtuous motive: And consequently the virtuous motive must be different from the regard to the virtue of the action. A virtuous motive is requisite to render an action virtuous. An action must be virtuous, before we can have a regard to its virtue. Some virtuous motive, therefore, must be antecedent to that regard. (T 3. 2.1.4)

Before you can perform a morally good action from a regard to its moral goodness, the action must already be good. What makes an action good is the goodness of its motive. This means that the first or original motive must be something other than the desire to perform the action because we see that it is good.

We can put Hume's point in terms of duties, which is more congenial to the rationalist outlook. Before we can act from the motive of duty, we need to know what our duties are. How do we know what they are? According to Hume, what makes an action a duty is that it is produced by a good motive. What motives are good? Imagine now that the only good motive is the motive of duty. If that were the only good motive, we would be in serious trouble because we would not know what our duties are. The motive of duty by itself cannot tell you what your duties are; by itself it has no content.

Hume concludes that "*no action can be virtuous, or morally good, unless there be in human nature some motive to produce it, distinct from the sense of its morality*" (T 3.2.1.7). This conclusion is the first premise in Hume's argument to show that justice is artificial. We need to keep in mind, however, that he is not claiming that people are never motivated by the motive of duty. Recall that he thinks that someone who happens to lack parental love, but still takes care of his children, may act from the motive of duty. But if Hume's argument is successful, the rationalist view that the motive of duty is original and primary is incoherent.

Justice arises artificially

Hume next asks us to consider an action required by justice. You borrow some money from someone, promising to pay it back in a few days. The agreed-upon day has arrived. What motive do you have to repay it? It is your duty to repay the loan, but if the circle argument is correct, your original motive is not the sense of duty. Anticipating his final position, Hume remarks that in a civilized society, once repaying loans has been established as a duty, the standard motive for any "honest" person is a regard for justice and an "abhorrence of villainy and knavery" (T 3.2.1.9).

What other motive could you have? Hume surveys a number of possibilities and rejects them all. One possible motive is the motive of self-interest when it "acts at its liberty"—without any restraints (T 3.2.1.10). According to this possibility, you repay the loan because it is in your interest to do so. He argues that this is not the original motive, because it sometimes prompts us to act unjustly. After all, if you do not repay the loan, you will be richer, and if the person who loaned you the money is not in a position to retaliate, you will not be harmed.

Another possible motive is a regard for the public interest—a concern for the good of society as a whole. You repay the loan because you care about the interests of society. Hume argues that this motive is not the original motive, since some individual acts of justice are harmful to the public interest. Consider a case in which there is a question about the legitimate heir to a fortune. One claimant would use it to fund medical research, while the other would fritter it away on worthless objects. If the second person turns out to be the legitimate heir, the public is the loser. There are also acts of justice where the public has no concern. If the loan was made in secret, the public has no interest in whether it is repaid or not. Moreover, when we pay our debts or keep our promises, we are not thinking about the good of society. That motive is "too remote and too sublime" (T 3.2.1.11). Finally, Hume denies that there is a love of humankind as such—Hutcheson's calm universal benevolence.

The final motive Hume considers is a regard for private benevolence—a concern for the interests of the party concerned. According to this possibility, you repay the loan because you love the person from whom you borrowed the money. But the lender may be your enemy or a vicious person who "deserves the hatred" of everyone (T 3.2.1.13). In cases such as these, your action is not motivated by your love and concern for the lender. In addition, private benevolence is not the original motive because justice is owed to everyone, but we are not required to be kind and generous to everyone.

Since the original motive for performing just actions is neither self-interest, nor a regard for public or private benevolence, there is no natural motive to justice. Hume therefore concludes that justice "arises artificially, tho' necessarily from education, and human conventions" (T 3.2.1.17).

In the next stage of his account of justice, Hume asks two different questions. The first concerns the *origin* of justice—the way in which the rules of justice come to be established by the "artifice" of human beings. What motivates human beings to develop a system of private property? The second question is why we morally approve of people who obey the rules of justice and disapprove of people who disobey them.

Hume's argument to show that justice is artificial leaves us with a puzzle: What is the *first* or *original* motive to justice? He will solve this puzzle in the course of answering his first question about the origin of justice. It is important to see that there is no motivational puzzle that arises in connection with the natural virtues. On his view, nature has supplied us with various motives—parental love, benevolence, and generosity—of which we approve. One of Hume's important insights is that nature has not provided human beings with all the motives they need to live together peacefully in a civilized society. Before we turn to his explanations of the origin of justice, we look in more detail at the standard interpretation of Hobbes' explanation of its origin—how his contemporaries and successors understood him—since Hume borrows from it.

The origin of justice: Hobbes

Rationalists and sentimentalists alike were repelled by Hobbes' picture of human nature and his account of moral and political obligation. His social contract theory fared much better, initiating a tradition that continues through Locke, Jean-Jacques Rousseau (1712–78), and Kant, to Rawls. The basic contractarian idea is that the laws that govern our association in society are ones that we voluntarily agree upon. People agree to enter society because it is to their advantage, and they consent to the laws that govern their cooperation. Hume takes over from Hobbes some of the questions and concerns of the modern social contract theory and to that extent belongs in that tradition. Both think that justice is a solution to a problem that arises because of our natural condition. Both argue that we agree to establish a system of justice because it is in our interest. Hume, however, will deny that the agreement consists in a promise or contract.

The problem, as Hobbes sees it, springs from two things: the nature of human beings, and the circumstances in which they find themselves, which he calls the state of nature. He begins by describing human nature. As we saw in Chapter 8, Hobbes portrays us as ruthlessly selfish and competitive, concerned above all with preserving ourselves and with increasing our power. Power is the means to self-preservation, but since power is secured only by more power, the search for it is bottomless. He also claims that all of our desires are self-interested, even such seemingly other-regarding desires as pity. Pity is grief for the misfortune of others that arises because we fear similar misfortunes might happen to us. While we seem to pity others, we are really grieving for ourselves. Human beings care only about themselves.

In chapter 13 of the *Leviathan*, Hobbes asks us to imagine what life would be like for selfish individuals who are concerned with preserving themselves and increasing their power in a state of nature, a pre-moral and pre-legal state. His starting point is that in the state of nature human beings are equal, both physically and mentally. The weakest is able to overpower the strongest by careful planning or by ganging up with others. Since prudence or foresight is due to experience, equal experience makes human beings equally prudent. He also argues that since everyone thinks they are smarter than everyone else, everyone is satisfied with their share of intelligence, which shows that it is equally distributed.

From this equality in power comes equality in hope: each of us expects that we will get what we want, but goods are scarce. If two people desire the same thing, but only one can have it, they will become enemies and will try to subdue or destroy each other. If I have something that others want, I know that they, either individually or in groups, will try to take it from me. But invaders are in the same situation: others will try to take their goods from them. All this makes us distrustful and wary of one another. The best defense, we realize, is to attack others before they attack us. We also are extremely jealous of our reputations, since the mere fact that others believe that I am weak decreases my power.

There are thus three principal causes of fighting: *competition*, in which we fight to gain control of other people and their material possessions; *wariness* or distrust of others, in which we fight to defend life and limb; and *glory*, in which we fight to maintain our reputation of being powerful.

Hobbes concludes that our natural condition is a "war ... of every man, against every man" (L 13.8; BM vol 1 36). In the state of nature, there is no industry, no navigation or agriculture, no civilization, art, literature, or society. We live in continual fear and danger of violent death. In one of his most famous phrases, he says that in the state of nature life is "solitary, poor, nasty, brutish and short" (L 13.9; BM vol 1 37).

In a remark that infuriated his successors, Hobbes claims that in the state of nature, nothing is wrong or unjust. There are no moral constraints and no one is under any moral obligation. Where there is no common power to keep us in line, there is no law, and where there is no law, there is no right or wrong, justice or injustice.

How do we get out of this horrible mess? Hobbes thinks what saves us is our fear of death, our desire for a pleasant life and our reason, which suggests a way out. The way out is to make a contract with one another. We agree to hand over our power and freedom to govern ourselves to a sovereign who has the power to make and enforce laws. These laws are called the laws of nature. They tell us to seek peace, since that is a means to our preservation, and to join a commonwealth, if others are willing to do so, since that is how we achieve peace. They also instruct us to keep our contracts, to be cooperative, to treat others as equals, and so on. Entering into a contract like this is the only way to ensure the peaceful conditions necessary for social life. It is in our interest to make this contract with one another.

According to Hobbes, both moral obligation and the political state come into being when the sovereign has the power to enforce the laws of nature. He enforces them with sanctions, by punishing violators. There is no assurance that others will obey the laws of nature unless there is a sovereign in place with the power to punish violators. Until there is a sovereign in place to enforce the laws of nature, there is no obligation to obey them. If you obey them all by yourself, you make yourself a victim of the ruthlessness of others. On Hobbes' view, acting morally requires that we obey the laws the sovereign makes and enforces, but the basis of morality is ultimately self-interest.

The origin of justice: Hume

The problem

Hume also thinks justice is a solution to a problem created by the natural condition in which we find ourselves. Drawing on Hume, Rawls calls these "the circumstances of justice" (TJ 3.22.1–2). In the *Treatise*, Hume appeals to three circumstances: our natural situation, the fact that our benevolence is originally confined to our family, and the fact that material goods are portable and scarce. The solution to the problem posed by these special circumstances is to establish property rights.

Nature, Hume says, seems to have been much more cruel to humans than to any of the other animals. We have numerous needs and wants, but few and slender natural resources to meet them. The needs and wants of the other animals, by contrast, are proportional to their natural means. A lion's appetites are voracious, but he has the physical strength and dexterity to satisfy them. A sheep's appetites are modest, but so are his natural resources. Only human beings have needs and wants that outstrip their natural resources. We must produce food necessary for our sustenance, make clothes, and build homes to protect us against inclement weather. We are not born with claws, fangs, or other natural means of defending ourselves from attacks by others. Generally speaking, we are needy but helpless creatures.

The remedy is to cooperate with one another. If a person works by himself, he faces three problems. He lacks the power to execute large projects—planting and harvesting a large field of crops. Since he has to do everything himself, he does not have the time to develop any specialized skills, let alone perfect them. He is especially vulnerable to misfortune. Accidents of nature may leave him devastated—a severe drought may destroy his crops. Cooperating with others allows us to overcome these problems. By joining forces, we are able to execute large projects. The division of labor allows individuals to develop and perfect their skills. I plant the harvest, you build barns, and someone else makes clothes. Mutual cooperation also provides some protection against misfortunes. Social cooperation is clearly to our advantage.

Fortunately, Hume says, human beings did not have to figure this out. The natural attraction between the sexes initially brings people together. Families are formed when they produce offspring and are sustained by the love parents naturally have for their children. Families, in turn, may unite with other families to form small societies. In this way, we come to experience the benefits of cooperation. Cooperation is natural to us.

There are two other circumstances, however, that pull us apart, one springing from our nature, the other from our outward circumstances. We are familiar with the problem arising from our nature. Our benevolence is originally confined to a narrow circle of people. We care about individuals in our extended family, but we are largely indifferent to people outside it. Instead of making us fit for a social life that extends beyond our family, our confined benevolence is contrary to it.

The fact that our benevolence is limited would not be a serious problem, if it were not for our outward circumstances. Of the three sorts of goods—goods of the mind, goods of the body, and material goods—only material possessions may be transferred to another "without suffering any loss or alteration" (T 3.2.2.7). Cars and computers may be taken from us intact, without being damaged. Moreover, material goods are also relatively scarce. There are not enough of them to meet everyone's needs and wants.

The problem is that since benevolence is confined and material goods are portable and scarce, I am tempted to take your possessions and give them to my family. But you are subject to the same temptation: you want to take my material goods and give them to your family. People are bound to fight over them and thus are in danger of losing the advantages of social cooperation.

To see this, suppose that we realize that we could produce more crops if we cooperate with one another than if we labor alone. We get together and plan and plant a large field of crops. However, since we are not able to produce enough crops to satisfy everyone, when harvest time comes, each of us plans on taking a larger portion for his family. Conflicts over possessions still arise and we continue to fight.

Hume agrees with Hobbes that if human nature were different or if our outward circumstances were different, justice would not be necessary. But he rejects the extreme selfishness Hobbes believes characterizes human beings. According to Hume, from the earliest stages of human history there has been cooperation among family members. What generates conflict is the fact that our affections originally center on them and material goods are portable and scarce. For Hobbes, competition over material goods spills over to where life and limb is at stake. For Hume, competition is limited to fighting over material possessions. Our natural state, according to him, is not nearly as brutish and nasty as Hobbes'.

The solution

The solution to the problem, Hume reminds us, is not to be found in our "uncultivated" ideas of morality, since we naturally approve of the partiality of our affections. Instead of providing a remedy for the biases in our affections, they only reinforce our partiality. The solution is not derived from nature, but from "*artifice*; or more properly speaking, nature provides a remedy in the judgment and understanding, for what is irregular and incommodious in the affections" (T 3.2.2.9).

Once we have experienced the advantages of social cooperation and understand that the main threat to social cooperation is the instability of material possessions, we seek a solution. We realize that we would be better off if we could prevent the conflicts that arise from competition over material goods. The way to do this is

> by a convention enter'd into by all the members of society to bestow stability on the possession of those external goods, and leave every one in the peaceable enjoyment of what he may acquire by his fortune and industry. (T 3.2.2.9)

The solution is to put material goods on the same footing as the goods of the mind and body. We do this by establishing property rights. We make rules that specify who has a right to what. We agree to follow the rules and to keep our hands off other people's property. Establishing who has a right to what will give rise to the moral obligation to respect the property rights of others.

Hume, like Hobbes, argues that having the practice of justice in place is in our interest. Our interests and those of our family are better promoted by observing the rules of justice than by consulting our interests in each and every case. Following the rules of justice makes it possible for us to live in a large and complex society and to reap the advantages of social cooperation. If we do not follow the rules of justice, we will be worse off, since we will continue to fight over material goods, thereby losing the benefits of social cooperation.

Hume, like Hobbes, also emphasizes the fact that the agreement must be reciprocal. It is in my interest to keep my hands off the property of others, provided that others agree to keep their hands off mine. It is not in my interest to agree unilaterally. If I agree and others do not, I would be leaving my possessions unprotected—ripe for the taking.

Hume realizes that the convention that gives rise to property rights is not "of the nature of a *promise*" or a contract, as Hobbes claims. Promising and making contracts are themselves practices that give rise to obligations and are therefore in as much need of explanation as the practice of justice and the obligation to which it gives rise. If a promise obligates us to keep our hands off other people's property, what obligates us to keep promises? The convention, Hume says, springs not from a promise but from a

> general sense of common interest; which all the members of the society express to one another, and which induces them to regulate their conduct by certain rules. I observe, that it will be for my interest to leave another in the possession of his goods, *provided* he will act in the same manner with regard to me. He is sensible of a like interest in the regulation of his conduct. When this common interest is mutually express'd, and is known to both, it produces a suitable resolution and behaviour. (T 3.2.2.10)

This is a kind of agreement even though there is no promise. The convention is similar to two people agreeing to row a boat in the same direction. They agree without promising or contracting.

Hume conceives of the convention that gives rise to property rights as something that evolves gradually as people come to experience the advantages that result from observing the rules of justice and the disadvantages that result from violating them. Significantly, he does not think that an enforcer with the power to punish violators is necessary to establish and maintain the practice of justice. Yet, he also thinks the usefulness of the rules of justice is so obvious that they were most likely first instituted in families. As he says, it would have been impossible for humans to remain for "any considerable time in that savage condition, which precedes society" (T 3.2.2.14). Our first state and condition is social.

The first motive to justice

Hume's initial problem was that he could not find the *first* or *original* motive to justice. His explanation of how the practice of justice arises reveals that it is self-interest. However, it is not the interest Hume rejected earlier—interest when it acts at liberty, which is often the source of injustice. I would be richer if I did not repay the loan. Let's call this sort of immediate interest—*direct* interest.

The interest that gets justice in place is different. It is an interest that regulates itself. "There is no passion, therefore, capable of controlling the interested affection, but the very affection itself, by an alteration of its direction"(T 3.2.2.13). Self-interest, in this second sense, redirects itself by taking a new object—the rules governing property rights. We make these rules because our interest is better satisfied when it is restrained than when we consult our interest in each and every case. Following the rules of justice make our possessions more secure, which makes it possible for us to live together peacefully in a large and complex society and to reap the advantages of social cooperation. Let's call this second type of interest—*redirected* interest. This is the first or original motive to justice.

Although the rules of justice are established by interest, their connection, as Hume notes, is "singular." Not every act of justice, when taken singly, is in our interest. It is easy to see how a person "may impoverish himself by a single instance of integrity, and have reason to wish that with regard to that single act, the laws of justice were for a moment suspended in the universe" (T 3.2.2.22). Returning the wallet I found to its owner may be the just thing to do, but it is not in my immediate interest. Nor is every act of justice in the public interest. Restoring a fortune to a miser or a drug addict may be the just thing to do, but the public is the loser. What is in our interest is the practice of justice. Each and every one of us is better off with the practice in place.

In the *Treatise*, Hume emphasizes the fact that when societies are small our interest in maintaining the system of justice is clear. We readily see the bad effects that result from violations of the rules of justice. In small societies, redirected self-interest is normally sufficient to motivate us to act justly. When a society becomes large and complex, our interest in the whole scheme or practice becomes more remote. We do not as readily see the harm that results from violations of the rules of justice and thus lose sight of our interest in maintaining the system of justice. In a large and complex society, it isn't obvious that injustice harms our interests. This is especially so in one case—when we would benefit from acting unjustly, say by stealing when we can get away with it.

On Hume's view, in a large and complex society, the standard motive for acting justly is the motive of duty. The motive of duty is more stable than the motive of redirected interest and is the motive we approve of most. In this way, Hume makes room for the motive of duty within a sentimentalist framework.

Justice as a virtue

Hume next turns to the question about why we approve of people who follow the rules of justice and disapprove of violators. In the second *Enquiry*, he makes it clear that at this point he parts company with Hobbes. In Section 5, "Why Utility Pleases," Hume reminds us that if we approve of actions because of their usefulness in producing certain effects, we must also approve of their effects. What is the basis of our approval of the effects?

Hume agrees with Hobbes that if justice is useful, it must serve somebody's interests. But he rejects what he thinks is Hobbes' view, namely, that we approve of people who obey the rules of justice because it is in our interest. Hume uses the same arguments we looked at in the last chapter to show that we do not approve of benevolence for self-interested reasons to show that we do not approve of justice for self-interested reasons either. If Hobbes' answer in terms of self-interest is excluded, he thinks only one possibility remains. It must be the "interest of those, who are served by the character or action approved of; and these we may conclude, however remote, are not totally indifferent to us" (EPM 5.1.15). We are not totally indifferent to the interests of others, because we have the capacity to sympathize with them. We approve of people who obey the rules of justice not because they benefit us, but because we sympathize with the benefits they bestow on others or society. Summarizing his position in the *Treatise*, Hume says

> Thus *self-interest* is the original motive to the *establishment* of justice: But a *sympathy* with the *public* interest is the source of the *moral* approbation, which attends this virtue. (T 3.2.2.24)

Hume explains our approval of the artificial virtue of justice by appealing to the same principles he used to explain our approval of the natural virtues.

The duties that arise from justice are owed to people not because of any special relationship we might have with them, but simply because they are our fellow citizens. Justice demands a kind of impartiality in our conduct that is not demanded in connection with the natural virtues. Keeping our hands off people's possessions, paying back loans, and returning lost wallets are duties owed to people, regardless of whether there are ties of personal affection.

The sensible knave

In Part 2 of the "Conclusion" of the second *Enquiry*, Hume raises a serious problem with his account of justice that also worried Hobbes. The problem is that while it is in our interest to have the practice of justice in place, it may not be in our interest to obey its rules in every case. This is the free rider problem. The free rider, whom Hume calls the sensible knave, wants to get the benefits that result from having a practice in place without having to always follow its rules. He knows that the only way to obtain the advantages of social cooperation is for the practice of justice to be in place. Most people will obey the rules of justice, so if he commits one act of injustice, the institution will not be in any danger of collapsing. Moreover, he may have the opportunity to commit an act of injustice that will benefit him greatly without getting caught. Why shouldn't he?

Hume confesses that if the sensible knave expects an answer, he is not sure there are any that will convince him.

If his heart rebel not against such pernicious maxims, if he feel
no reluctance to the thoughts of villainy or baseness, he has
indeed lost a considerable motive to virtue ... (EPM 9.2.23)

He continues by saying that for most of us, our abhorrence
of "treachery and roguery" is so strong that it overrides any
thoughts about the advantages of acting unjustly. "Inward peace
of mind, consciousness of integrity, a satisfactory review of our
own conduct" are important ingredients of happiness and are
"cherished and cultivated by every honest man" who acknowledges
their importance (EPM 9.23). Having peace of mind is one thing
that makes us happy. If we acknowledge that we ought to obey the
rules of justice, we will have peace of mind only by acting justly.

It turns out that, in the sort of case the sensible knave has in
mind, the motive of duty is the only available motive. Most of
us are honest people and have this motive. The problem with the
sensible knave, however, is that he lacks it. There is still considerable disagreement about how to understand Hume's response to
the sensible knave and whether it is adequate.

Hume's account of justice remains deeply influential. Philosophers
continue to this day to debate when the motive of duty is appropriate and when spontaneous, natural motives are appropriate.
They also worry about the free rider problem. Hume's sketch of the
evolution of social cooperation has inspired contemporary evolu-
tionary accounts of social cooperation. His explanation of justice
was important to Rawls, especially in his masterpiece *A Theory of
Justice*.

11

Philosophy of religion

Hume wrote forcefully and incisively on almost every central question in the philosophy of religion. Add up the pages he devoted to these issues and their total exceeds the space he gave to any other single topic. He contributed to ongoing debates about the reliability of reports of miracles, the immateriality and immortality of the soul, the morality of suicide, and the natural history of religion, among others. All this work excited heated reactions in his day, but his arguments outlived those local disputes. They still figure centrally in our discussions of these issues today.

Hume's greatest achievement in the philosophy of religion is the *Dialogues concerning Natural Religion*. This work is generally regarded as one of the most important and influential contributions to this area of philosophy. While all Hume's books provoked controversy, the *Dialogues* were thought to be so inflammatory that his friends persuaded him to withhold them from publication until after his death.

The *Dialogues* are a sustained and penetrating critical examination of a prominent argument from analogy for the existence and nature of God: the argument from design. The argument from design attempts to establish that the order we find in the universe is so like the order we find in the products of human artifice that it too must be the product of an intelligent designer.

Since the idea of intelligent design is still hotly debated, the *Dialogues* are clearly relevant today. But they were even more relevant to the eighteenth-century British debate about *natural religion*, where the argument from design took center stage.

Natural religion or *natural theology*, as those terms were used in this period, concerns questions about whether claims about God's existence and his various natural and moral attributes can be established solely by considering evidence from the natural world and reasoning about it. So understood, natural religion contrasts with *revealed religion*, which takes the central claims of a religious view to be based on *revelation*—a direct encounter with God or one of his delegates, or through literal reading of scripture.

In Chapter 7, we saw that Hume's dissolution of the longstanding controversy about liberty and necessity provides a case study of his philosophical project at work, where his contributions to the debates about causation and the foundations of ethics converge. In this brief final chapter, we will see that the *Dialogues* not only illustrate his philosophical project, but also exhibit how his conclusions from all three debates come together.

The characters

The *Dialogues* record a conversation between three characters. *Cleanthes*, a self-proclaimed "experimental theist," offers the argument from design as an empirical proof of God's existence and nature (DCNR 5.2). *Demea* opposes him, maintaining that the argument's merely probable conclusion demeans God's mystery and majesty. He believes that God's nature is completely inscrutable. Cleanthes dubs Demea a *mystic*, while Demea derides Cleanthes' *anthropomorphism*—his human-centered bias in comparing the creator of the universe to a human mind.

Cleanthes and Demea represent the central positions in the eighteenth-century natural religion debate. Cleanthes embodies its dominant, progressive strain, which consisted primarily of theologians in the British Royal Society. They were fascinated by probability and the previous century's impressive successes in experimental natural philosophy. Convinced that the new science was witness to God's providence, they rejected traditional a priori proofs, which purported to demonstrate God's existence with mathematical certainty and without appeal to experience. Instead, they used the order and regularity they found in the universe to construct a probabilistic argument for a divine designer.

Holdouts clung to demonstrative proof in science and theology against the rising tide of probability. Demea is the champion of these conservative traditionalists. Since he trots out a lame version of Samuel Clarke's cosmological argument in Part 9, some have thought that Hume models Demea on him. But Demea lacks Clarke's rigid rationalism. It is more likely that he epitomizes a group of minor theologians such as William Law and William King, who were right-wing opponents of the design argument. They insisted on God's incomprehensibility and used a priori arguments only when they absolutely needed an argument.

There was no genuinely skeptical presence in the eighteenth-century natural religion debate. This makes *Philo*, who both Cleanthes and Demea characterize as a skeptic, the ringer in the conversation. Although all three characters say very Humean things at one time or another, Philo's views are consistently the closest to Hume's. Philo's form of skepticism is the *mitigated skepticism* of the first *Enquiry*, which makes him the logical candidate to be Hume's spokesman. That this is indeed the case will emerge clearly as we look at the details of the conversation, where Philo's argument conforms closely to Hume's project.

As the *Dialogues* begin, all three characters agree that their subject is God's *nature*, since everyone grants that he *exists*. Parts 1–8 concern God's *natural attributes*, his omnipotence, omniscience, and providence, while Parts 10 and 11 consider his *moral attributes*, his benevolence and righteousness.

God's natural attributes

Demea holds that God is completely unknown and incomprehensible. All we can say is that God is a being without restriction, absolutely infinite and universal. Cleanthes is adamant that the argument from design establishes all of God's traditional attributes. Natural objects and human artifacts like tables and chairs resemble one another, so by analogy, their causes also resemble each other. God is therefore like a human mind, only very much greater in every respect.

Demea objects that the argument's conclusion is only probable, but Philo responds that the real problem is that the analogy is so weak. He launches a battery of arguments to show just how weak it is. The dissimilarities between human artifacts like a table or a chair and the universe are more striking than their similarities. We only experience a tiny part of the universe for a short time, and much of what we do experience is unknown to us. How can we legitimately infer anything about remote parts of the universe, much less the universe as a whole?

Philo, however, moves quickly away from chipping at the argument's *strength* to questioning the *intelligibility* of its conclusion. We have no *experience* of the origin of a universe. Since causal inference requires a basis in experienced constant conjunction between two kinds of things, how can we legitimately draw any conclusion whatsoever about the origin of the universe? Does it even require a cause? One or many? Does the cause of the universe itself require a cause? The problem, then, is not just that the analogy is weak; the real problem is that it attempts to take us beyond the range of our faculties.

Meanwhile, Demea derides Cleanthes' *anthropomorphism* while remaining smugly satisfied with what Cleanthes disparagingly calls his *mysticism*. The barbs they throw at each other, and the speeches Philo goads them to make, help create a dilemma that Philo is using them to construct. He directs the dilemma at Cleanthes, but it affects both characters, although Demea is slow to realize this. He thinks Philo is in league with him in detailing the problems with Cleanthes' anthropomorphism.

Challenging Cleanthes to explain what he means by God's mind, Philo pushes him to admit that he means "a mind like the human." Cleanthes takes the bait and responds, "I know of no other" (DCNR 5.4). He argues that mystics like Demea are really no better than *atheists*, since they make God so remote and incomprehensible that he bears no resemblance to human characteristics. Philo adds that although we regard God as perfect, perfection as we understand it is relative, not absolute, so we cannot conclude that we grasp God's perfections. And since all God's attributes involve perfection—perfect knowledge, perfect power, perfect goodness—we should not think that *any* of his attributes resemble or are even analogous to our perfections, since He is infinitely superior to us in every way. But this means that we do not know what we are talking about when we talk about God using the familiar terms we apply to human minds.

Demea adds that giving God human characteristics, even if they are greatly magnified, denies him attributes theists have always ascribed to him. How can an anthropomorphic God have the *unity, simplicity,* and *immutability* of the God of traditional theism?

Philo continues to detail just how *inconvenient* the anthropomorphism Cleanthes accepts really is. If he remains committed to the argument from design, he must be committed to a God who is finite in all respects. But what does it mean to say that God is finitely perfect? Once you admit that God is finite, you have opened a can of worms, for there are all sorts of equally probable alternatives to intelligent design. Why think that the universe is more like a human artifact than an animal or a vegetable?

To illustrate, Philo throws out a number of outlandish alternative hypotheses. For instance, if you were a spider on a planet of spiders, wouldn't you naturally believe that a giant spider spun an immense web to create the world?

Cleanthes' design hypothesis is so underdetermined by the evidence that the only reasonable approach is to abandon any attempt to adjudicate among it and its many alternatives. Total suspense of judgment is the only reasonable response. Trying to address the issue demands that we go beyond the bounds of anything to which we can give specific content.

The dilemma Philo has constructed encapsulates the issues about the content of the idea of God that is central to the critical aspect of Hume's project in the *Dialogues*. If you accept that God's attributes are infinite, you are using ordinary terms without their ordinary meaning, so that they do not have any clear meaning. If you deny God's infinity, you can give him understandable attributes, but only because they are amplified human characteristics. The closer Cleanthes comes to regarding God's mind as like a human mind, the closer he comes to regarding God's attributes as being like human attributes, and the less Godlike his "God" is. We can only give the idea of God intelligible content at the perilously high cost of denying that he is really God. To do so is to abandon God for some kind of superhero.

At the end of Part 8, which concludes their discussion of God's natural attributes, Demea still thinks Philo and he are working together. He remains clueless about Philo's strategy until the very end of Part 11, when he finally realizes that he too is caught in the trap Philo has sprung.

Demea offers an a priori alternative to the design argument in Part 9. As noted earlier, it is an extremely abbreviated, watered-down version of Clarke's cosmological argument. Although Cleanthes quickly scotches his lame efforts, Part 9 serves as an interlude between the previous discussion of God's *natural attributes* and the consideration of his *moral attributes* in Parts 10 and 11.

God's moral attributes

Demea begins the discussion in Part 10. Attempting to save face from his recent drubbing, he suggests that we do not accept the truths of religion as a result of reasoning, but from what we *feel* when confronted with how helpless and miserable we are. Religion is based on feelings of fear and anxiety that arise from awareness of our "imbecility and misery" (DCNR 10.1). Our forms of worship are attempts to appease unknown powers that oppress and torment us.

Philo joins in, claiming he is convinced that "the best and indeed the only method of bringing everyone to a due sense of religion is by just representations of the misery and wickedness of men" (DCNR 10.2). They proceed with a joint litany of the misery and melancholy of the human condition, topping each other with catalogues of woes. Demea does not realize that Philo may mean very different things by "just representation" and "due sense of religion" than he does, so he fails to realize that Philo is just egging him on.

Philo maintains that we cannot evade the facts of disease, famine, and pestilence, except by "apologies, which still farther aggravate the charge" (DCNR 10.16). These apologies are *theodicies*—systematic attempts to reconcile God's goodness with the existence of evil. Demea is also scornful of theodicies, blissfully unaware that all too soon he will be offering his own.

Cleanthes finally breaks in to say that *he* does not feel oppressively anxious or miserable, and hopes that anguish is not so common as they claim. But *hoping* that the extent of human misery is not so widespread is not the same as *proving* that it is. Cleanthes is on weak ground. Philo capitalizes on it, challenging Cleanthes to explain how God's mercy and benevolence can possibly resemble human mercy and benevolence. Given God's omnipotence, whatever he wills happens, but neither humans nor animals are happy, so God presumably does not will their happiness.

Cleanthes—"smiling"—grants that if Philo can *prove* that humankind is "unhappy or corrupted," he will have succeeded at doing in religion (DCNR 10.28). Cleanthes is smiling because he thinks he finally has Philo on the ropes. In forcing a skeptic to prove a positive thesis, he must not only succeed at a difficult task, but will violate his skepticism in the process. Cleanthes fails to realize that Philo will make his case without needing to prove anything, nor does he realize that *he* will soon be the one who needs a proof.

Demea objects that Cleanthes exaggerates the dire consequences of acknowledging the human condition, and, despite his earlier vehement rejection of theodicies, offers his own. Sometimes called "the porch view," Demea's theodicy compares our experience of the world to the world as a whole, including the afterlife, to trying to determine the structure of a large building from what little we can see from its porch. From our perspective, we suffer, but from a longer view we either don't suffer at all, or our suffering is for our greater good or for the greater good of the world.

Cleanthes retorts that Demea denies the facts, and offers only empty hypotheses, which, if intelligible at all, could only establish their bare possibility, but never their reality. The only way to respond to challenges to God's benevolence is to deny that the human condition is really so miserable.

Cleanthes has now put himself in the position in which he thought he had put Philo. He must establish that the facts are as he claims, and Philo is quick to stress how difficult this will be. By resting his case on such an uncertain point, any conclusion he draws will be equally uncertain.

Philo then ups the ante by granting for the sake of argument that human happiness exceeds human misery. But if God is infinitely powerful, wise, and good, why is there any misery at all? There is no answer that preserves all God's attributes, except to grant that the subject exceeds all human capacity.

Philo, however, refrains from pressing the question of *intelligibility*. He is more interested in building an even stronger case against Cleanthes' inference to God's *benevolence*. Raising the ante higher still, he grants that pain and suffering are *compatible* with God's infinite power and goodness. Cleanthes, however, must prove from the "mixed and confused phenomena" that God's benevolence is *actual*, not merely *possible*. Doing so is doubly difficult, since any inference from finite to infinite is shaky at best, even when the data are "pure and unmixed" (DCNR 10.35).

Philo concludes by admitting, with less-than-complete sincerity, that while he was hard pressed to make his case against Cleanthes when the discussion concerned God's natural attributes, where his moral attributes are concerned, he is at ease. He challenges Cleanthes "to tug the labouring oar" and explain how he can infer God's moral attributes from the facts about the human condition (DCNR 10.36).

Cleanthes "tugs," but only for one short paragraph. He admits that if we go beyond their usual meanings when we apply human terms to God, what we say is indeed unintelligible. Abandoning all human analogy is thus to abandon natural religion, but preserving it makes it impossible to reconcile evil with an infinite God.

Cleanthes realizes he has painted himself into a corner, but once again he thinks there is a way out. Abandon God's infinity; think of him as "finitely perfect." Then "benevolence, regulated by wisdom, and limited by necessity, may produce just such a world as the present" (DCNR 11.1).

Cleanthes does not realize that his new theory is worse than his old one. He also does not seem to remember Philo's earlier question about what "finitely perfect" might possibly mean. Instead of God, he is now committed to some kind of superhero. Besides, the story he is telling is itself a theodicy. His superhero's limitations explain why he cannot eliminate evil, or create an evil-free world.

In any case, Cleanthes is no better off than he was before. Conjectures may show that the data are *consistent* with the idea of God, but they are never sufficient to prove that he actually exists.

Philo then proceeds to outline four possible hypotheses about the cause of the universe: it is perfectly good; it is perfectly evil; it is both good and evil; it is neither good nor evil. Given the evil we know exists, the data is at best *mixed*, so it cannot establish either of the first two hypotheses. The regularity and uniformity of the general laws we find in experience is sufficient to discount the third, so the fourth seems the most probable. On that hypothesis, the cause of the universe is entirely indifferent to the amount of good and evil in the world.

These points about *natural* evil also apply to *moral* evil. We have no more reason to think that God's righteousness resembles human righteousness than we have to think that his benevolence resembles human benevolence. We have even less reason, in fact, since moral evil outweighs moral goodness more than natural evil outweighs natural goodness.

In addition, Cleanthes' new form of anthropomorphism is saddled with tracing moral evil back to God. Since every effect must have a cause, either the chain of causes goes back infinitely, or it stops with the original principle that is the ultimate cause of all things—God.

At this point, Demea, who has become increasingly agitated during Philo's speech, interrupts. He has finally realized that the case Philo is making cuts against his own view as much as it cuts against Cleanthes'. Although it might appear that Demea can retreat to some form of the theodicy he sketched earlier, the extent to which Philo's argument upsets him suggests that he now realizes it is inadequate. If he leans on the mystery-mongering he has professed until now, Philo has shown that, because of its lack of specific content, it does not point exclusively to a good God. It may just as well commit him to a supreme being who is "beyond good and evil" and is totally indifferent to morality. Commitment without content turns out to be no commitment at all. Demea realizes this, dimly at least, as he leaves the conversation.

The conclusion: part 12

With Demea's departure, Cleanthes and Philo are left to finish the conversation. Their tone is conciliatory, so conciliatory in fact that Philo says he must "confess" that although he is less cautious about natural religion than any other subject,

> no one has a deeper sense of religion impressed on his mind, or pays more profound adoration to the divine being, as he discovers himself to reason, in the inexplicable contrivance and artifice of nature. (DCNR 12.2)

Philo's "confession" paves the way for a blockbuster that has puzzled generations of readers. Philo seems to reverse field, apparently recanting what he has argued for so forcefully. He grants Cleanthes that "a purpose, an intention, a design, strikes everywhere the most careless, the most stupid thinker" (DCNR 12.2).

His remarks are, however, by no means straightforward. Some take Philo—and, by implication, Hume—to be outing himself as a closet theist. Others conclude that, since he holds all the cards at this point, he can easily afford to be conciliatory. Read ironically, Philo could be saying that while "careless and stupid" observers are struck by purpose, intention, and design in the universe, careful, critical, intelligent ones are not. But there is no need to force the irony here. Read straight, nature's "contrivance and artifice" is "inexplicable" precisely because reason can discover nothing about God's natural or moral attributes. Everyone—even the stupid and careless—can see that the parts of animals and plants have *functions*, and so can easily understand why "an anatomist, who discovered a new organ or canal, would never be satisfied until he had also discovered its use and intention" (DCNR 12.2).

Recognizing that an organism's parts have *uses—functions—* says nothing about whether their uses or functions are due to the plan of a designer, so Philo's acknowledgment of them implies nothing about whether he now accepts the design hypothesis. In fact, what he says here does no more than reiterate his position in Part 8—that function alone is no proof of divine design:

> It is in vain … to insist upon the uses of the parts of animals or vegetables and their curious adjustment to each other. I would fain know how an animal could subsist, unless its parts were so adjusted? (DCNR 8.9)

No one should deny design *in this sense*, so long as they do so "without any religious purpose" (DCNR 12.2). Far from reversing himself, then, Philo's position is continuous with the line he has taken throughout the *Dialogues*.

At this point, Philo provides a diagnosis of the dispute about design. While the works of nature do bear "a great analogy" to the products of human artifice, as its proponents claim, there are also considerable differences. He suspects that this may be the source of the intractability of the controversy, which suggests that it may be at bottom "somewhat of a dispute of words" (DCNR 12.6).

But verbal disputes can be resolved—or *dissolved*—by providing clear definitions. As we saw in the dispute over liberty and necessity in Chapter 7, applying Hume's account of definition provided a constructive solution to that longstanding controversy. However, the dilemma about the content of our idea of God that Philo has constructed clearly implies that a similar constructive solution is not possible here.

Philo explains why only a critical solution is possible by offering a deeper diagnosis of the problem. Although superficially the dispute may appear to be merely verbal, it is in fact "still more incurably ambiguous." He explains that

> there is a species of controversy, which, from the very nature of language and of human ideas, is involved in perpetual ambiguity, and can never, by any precaution or any definitions, be able to reach a reasonable certainty or precision. These are the controversies concerning the degrees of any quality or circumstance. (DCNR 12.7)

This is exactly what the dispute over intelligent design is about. Analogies are always matters of degree, and the degrees of the qualities involved in the design argument are not capable of exact measurement. The controversy thus "admits not of any precise meaning, nor consequently of any determination" (DCNR 12.7). The dispute about design is actually *worse* than a verbal dispute.

That is why anyone, even an atheist, can say, with equal plausibility, that "the rotting of a turnip, the generation of an animal, and the structure of human thought" all "probably bear some remote analogy to each other" (DCNR 12.7). That is why Philo, without renouncing any of his previous claims, can assent to the "somewhat ambiguous, at least undefined," and, as we have seen, *indefinable* proposition into which "the whole of natural theology ... resolves itself ... *that the cause or causes of order in the universe probably bear some remote analogy to human intelligence*" (DCNR 12.33).

Anything is like anything else in *some* remote respect. So the ordering principle of the universe, if indeed there is one, can be *absolutely anything*.

If this is all there is to "the whole of natural theology," then we can certainly conclude that the argument's conclusion has no religiously significant content. But it has no religiously significant content because Philo's critique has drained it of any content whatsoever. Cleanthes' design hypothesis is not just false—it is unintelligible.

The conversation began with all three participants agreeing that their topic was to discuss only God's *nature*, not his *existence*. As we conclude, it is no longer clear that those questions are really so distinct as originally assumed. We do not know what we are talking about when we talk about a God whose nature is inconceivable, incomprehensible, indeterminate, and indefinable. What, then, are we to make of the claim about his existence?

The *Dialogues* draw out the consequences of Hume's statement, at the beginning of the first *Enquiry*, that "the idea of God, as meaning an infinitely intelligent, wise, and good Being, arises from reflecting on the operations of our own mind, and augmenting, without limit, those qualities of goodness and wisdom" (EHU 2.6). If we insist on "augmenting without limit," we let loose the moorings that give intelligible content to God's goodness, wisdom, and intelligence. If we stop short of the limit, we may have content, but we have also lost God.

FURTHER READING

Primary sources: works by Hume

Many editions of Hume's works are available, including those in the public domain. Here are some standard editions.

A Treatise of Human Nature (1739–40), L. A. Selby-Bigge and P. H. Nidditch (eds), Oxford: Clarendon Press, 1975

A Treatise of Human Nature (1739–40), D. F. Norton and M. Norton (eds), Oxford University Press, 2000

An Enquiry concerning Human Understanding (1748), in *Enquiries concerning Human Understanding and concerning the Principles of Morals* (1975), L. A. Selby-Bigge and P. H. Nidditch (eds), Oxford: Clarendon Press

An Enquiry concerning Human Understanding (1748), T. L. Beauchamp ed., Oxford: Oxford University Press, 1999

An Enquiry concerning the Principles of Morals (1751), in *Enquiries concerning Human Understanding and concerning the Principles of Morals* (1975), L. A. Selby-Bigge and P. H. Nidditch (eds), Oxford: Clarendon Press

An Enquiry concerning the Principles of Morals (1751), T. L. Beauchamp ed., Oxford: Oxford University Press, 1998

The History of England, 6 vols (1754–61), W. B. Todd ed., Indianapolis: Liberty Classics, 1983

A Dissertation on the Passions and The Natural History of Religion (1757), T. L. Beauchamp ed., Oxford: Clarendon Press, 2007

Dialogues concerning Natural Religion (1779), D. Coleman ed., Cambridge: Cambridge University Press, 2007

Essays Moral, Political, and Literary (1777), E. Miller ed., Indianapolis: Liberty Fund, 1987

Primary sources: seventeenth- and eighteenth-century philosophers

Descartes, R. (1984), *The Philosophical Works of Descartes*, 2 vols, J. Cottingham, R. Stoothoff and D. Murdoch (trans), Cambridge: Cambridge University Press (includes Descartes' *Meditations*)

Hobbes, T. (1651), *Leviathan*, E. Curley ed., Indianapolis: Hackett Publishing Company, 1994

Hutcheson, F. (1725), *An Inquiry into the Original of our Ideas of Beauty and Virtue*, W. Leidhold ed., Indianapolis: Liberty Fund, 2008

—(1728), *An Essay on the Nature and Conduct of the Passions and Affections with Illustrations on the Moral Sense*, A. Garrett ed., Indianapolis: Liberty Fund, 2002

Locke, J. (1689), *An Essay concerning Human Understanding*, P. H. Nidditch ed., Oxford: Clarendon Press, 1975

Mandeville, B. (1714), "An Enquiry into the Origin of Moral Virtue," in *The Fable of the Bees or, Private Vices, Publick Benefits*, 2 vols, F. B. Kaye ed., Indianapolis: Liberty Classics, 1988

Newton, I. (2004), *Philosophical Writings*, A. Janiak ed., Cambridge: Cambridge University Press

Raphael, D. D. ed. (1991), *British Moralists 1650–1800*, 2 vols, Indianapolis: Hackett Publishing Company

Schneewind, J. B. ed. (1990), *Moral Philosophy from Montaigne to Kant*, 2 vols, Cambridge: Cambridge University Press

Secondary literature on Hume

There is a great deal of work on various aspects of Hume's philosophy and its relation to problems in contemporary philosophy.

Árdal, P. (1966), *Passion and Value in Hume's Treatise*, Edinburgh: Edinburgh University Press

Baier, A. C. (1991), *A Progress of Sentiments*, Cambridge: Harvard University Press

Beauchamp, T. L. and Rosenberg, A. (1981), *Hume and the Problem of Causation*, New York: Oxford University Press

Bennett, J. (2001), *Learning from Six Philosophers*, 2 vols, Oxford: Clarendon Press

Blackburn, S. (1998), *Ruling Passion: A Theory of Practical Reasons*, Oxford: Oxford University Press

—(2008), *How to Read Hume*, London: Granta

Buckle, S. (2001), *Hume's Enlightenment Tract: The Unity and Purpose of* An Enquiry concerning Human Understanding, Oxford: Clarendon Press

Cohon, R. ed. (2001), *Hume: Moral and Political Philosophy*, Aldershot: Ashgate

—(2008), *Hume's Morality: Feeling and Fabrication*, Oxford: Oxford University Press

Fogelin, R. J. (1985), *Hume's Scepticism in the* Treatise of Human Nature, London: Routledge and Kegan Paul

Forbes, D. (1975), *Hume's Philosophical Politics*, Cambridge: Cambridge University Press

Frasca-Spada, M. and Kail, P. J. E. (eds) (2005), *Impressions of Hume*, Oxford: Clarendon Press

Garrett, D. (1997), *Cognition and Commitment in Hume's Philosophy*, Oxford: Oxford University Press

Harris, J. A. (2005), *Of Liberty and Necessity: The Free Will Debate in Eighteenth-Century British Philosophy*, Oxford: Clarendon Press

Harrison, J. (1981), *Hume's Theory of Justice*, Oxford: Oxford University Press

Loeb, L. E. (2002), *Stability and Justification in Hume's* Treatise, Oxford: Oxford University Press

Mackie, J. L. (1980), *Hume's Moral Theory*, London: Routledge

Millican, P. ed. (2002), *Reading Hume on Human Understanding*, Oxford: Clarendon Press

Mossner, E. C. (1954), *The Life of David Hume*, London: Nelson

Norton, D. F. and Taylor, J. (eds) (2009), *The Cambridge Companion to Hume*, Cambridge: Cambridge University Press

Owen, D. (2000), *Hume's Reason*, Oxford: Oxford University Press

Penelhum, T. (1975), *Hume: Philosophers in Perspective*, London: Macmillan

Radcliffe, E. S. ed. (2008), *A Companion to Hume*, Malden, MA: Blackwell

Read, R. and Richman, K. A. (eds) (2000), *The New Hume Debate*, New York: Routledge

Russell, P. (1995), *Freedom and Moral Sentiment*, New York: Oxford University Press

Schneewind, J. B. (1998), *The Invention of Autonomy*, Cambridge: Cambridge University Press

Smith, N. K. (1941), *The Philosophy of David Hume*, London: Macmillan

Stewart, M. A. and Wright, J. P. (eds) (1994), *Hume and Hume's Connexions*, Edinburgh: Edinburgh University Press

Stroud, B. (1977), *Hume*, London: Routledge

Traiger, S. ed. (2006), *The Blackwell Guide to Hume's* Treatise, Malden, MA: Blackwell

Tweyman, S. ed. (1995), *David Hume: Critical Assessments*, 6 vols, London: Routledge
Wright, J. P. (1983), *The Sceptical Realism of David Hume*, Minneapolis: University of Minnesota Press

Bibliographical studies

Useful bibliographies of work on Hume include:

Hall, R. (1978), *Fifty Years of Hume Scholarship: A Bibliographical Guide*, Edinburgh: Edinburgh University Press

Hall also prepared annual bibliographies of the Hume literature for *Hume Studies*, a journal specializing in work on Hume, for the years 1977–86: these bibliographies appeared in the November issues of that journal from 1978 to 1988.

Hume Studies revived the practice of including bibliographies with its November 1994 issue, which contained a comprehensive bibliography of the Hume literature from 1986–93 by William Edward Morris. Subsequent volumes contain annual supplements to this bibliography, by Morris, and more recently, James Fieser.

BIBLIOGRAPHY

(Publication details of books mentioned in the text)

Allestree, R. (1704), *The Whole Duty of Man*. Google e-books, 2009

Cicero, M. T. (1856), *Three Books of Offices*, Edmonds, C. R. (trans), Google e-books, 2006

Clarke, S. (1706), *Discourse concerning the Unchangeable Obligations of Natural Religion*, selections in D. D. Raphael, *British Moralists 1650–1800*, 2 vols, Indianapolis: Hackett Publishing Company, 1991

Darwin, C. (1859), *The Origin of Species by Means of Natural Selection*, London: John Murray

Descartes, R. (1640), *Meditations* in *The Philosophical Works of Descartes*, 2 vols, J. Cottingham, R. Stoothoff, and D. Murdoch (trans), Cambridge: Cambridge University Press, 1984

Galileo, G. (1623), *The Assayer*, S. Drake (trans) in *The Controversy of the Comets of 1618*, Philadelphia: The University of Pennsylvania Press, 1960

Hobbes, T. (1651), *Leviathan*, E. Curley ed., Indianapolis: Hackett Publishing Company, 1994

Hooke, R. (1665), *Micrographia*, Project Gutenberg, 2005 [EBook #15491]

Hume, D. (1739–40), *A Treatise of Human Nature*, Project Gutenberg, 2010 [EBook #4705]

—(1740), *An Abstract of A Treatise of Human Nature, 1740*, reprinted with an introduction by J. M. Keynes and P Sraffa, Cambridge: Cambridge University Press, 1938

—(1748/1777), *An Enquiry concerning Human Understanding*, reprint of the edition of 1777, Project Gutenberg, 2006 [EBook #9662]

—(1751/1777), *An Enquiry concerning the Principles of Morals*, reprint of the edition of 1777, Project Gutenberg, 2010 [EBook #4320]. Also contains Hume's "Advertisement"

—(1754–61), *The History of England*, 6 vols, W. B. Todd ed., Indianapolis: Liberty Classics, 1983

—(1757) *A Dissertation on the Passions* and *The Natural History of Religion*, T. L. Beauchamp ed., Oxford: Clarendon Press, 2007

—(1777), *Essays, Moral, Political, and Literary*, E. F. Miller ed., Indianapolis: Liberty Classics, 1987. Includes Hume's posthumous essays, "Of Suicide" and "Of the Immortality of the Soul"

—(1779), *Dialogues concerning Natural Religion*, D. Coleman ed., Cambridge: Cambridge University Press, 2007

—(1932), *Letters of David Hume*, vol 1, J. T. Y. Greig ed., Oxford: Clarendon Press. Contains Hume's autobiographical essay, "My Own Life" (1776)

Hutcheson, F. (1728), *An Essay on the Nature and Conduct of the Passions and Affections with Illustrations on the Moral Sense*, A. Garrett ed., Indianapolis: Liberty Fund, 2002

—(1725), *An Inquiry into the Original of our Ideas of Beauty and Virtue*, W. Leidhold ed., Indianapolis: Liberty Fund, 2008

Locke, J. (1689), *An Essay concerning Human Understanding*, P. H. Nidditch ed., Oxford: Clarendon Press, 1975

Malebranche, N. (1674–5), *The Search After Truth*, T. M. Lennon ed., Columbus: The Ohio State University Press, 1980

Mandeville, B. (1714), "An Enquiry into the Origin of Moral Virtue," in *The Fable of the Bees or, Private Vices, Publick Benefits*, vol 1, F. B. Kaye ed., Indianapolis: Liberty Classics, 1988

Newton, I. (2004), *Philosophical Writings*, A. Janiak ed., Cambridge: Cambridge University Press

Raphael, D. D. ed. *British Moralists 1650–1800*, 2 vols, Indianapolis: Hackett Publishing Company, 1991

Rawls, J. (1971), *A Theory of Justice*, Harvard: Harvard University Press

Wollaston, W. (1724), *Religion of Nature Delineated*, New York: Garland Publishing, 1978

INDEX